KILLER
church

WHY SOME JUST SURVIVE AND OTHERS
THRIVE IN THE PRESENCE OF GOD

NATHAN FINOCHIO

Published in association with Per Capita Publishing, a division of Content Capital®.

ISBN 13: 978-1-954020-29-0 (Paperback)
ISBN 13: 978-1-954020-33-7 (Ebook)

Library of Congress Cataloging-in-Publication Data
Names: Finochio, Nathan, author.
Title: Killer Church / Nathan Finochio
Description: First Edition | Texas: Per Capita Publishing (2022)
Identifiers: LCCN 2022908872 (print)

First Edition

This book is dedicated to Jasmine, the wife of my youth,
who causes theory to become experience.

CONTENTS

SIDE A

INTERLUDE

SIDE B

SIDE A

Chapter One

AVOCADO TOAST

According to a US Census Bureau in 2009,[1] the average marriage lasts for eight years. My theory for this is that we are master manipulators who project onto each other the idealized spouse—we are so infatuated with the person that we fantasize they possess important qualities, even though a second careful look would prove otherwise.

So we believe our lies and theirs (dating is a bunch of lies) and jump into the eternal flame like the idiots we are. But the infatuation begins to wear off as time goes by, and we being to take second and third glances. We begin to notice that they in fact do not embody our projected fantasies. We begin to say things like, "Who are you? You never told me you're like this!"

Year eight is the year we divorce because we can no longer project and thus control them. We are forced to

1.https://www.census.gov/newsroom/releases/archives/marital_status_living_ar-rangements/cb11-90.html#:~:text=Other%20highlights%3A,was%20shorter%20%E2%80%94%20about%20seven%20years (accessed March 2, 2022).

reckon with the actual personality and interests of the person we have married—a person we have nothing in common with (because they aren't us, they're a different human—imagine that).

In year eight, we have two choices: the decision to get to know this strange person whom we don't understand with a childlike curiosity so that true intimacy can be achieved, or the decision to divorce this person we don't know because we are no longer married to the fantasy that never existed in the first place.

My wife and I are in year eight.

And we've decided that divorce isn't an option, murder is too risky, and all that's left to do is find out who in God's green earth we are married to.

I'm trying to figure this Jasmine girl out all over again like a Raymond Chandler private detective. In my mind, I'm a moody reluctant Humphrey Bogart trying to crack the code on this mysterious and elusive Bacall character. I'm putting the puzzle together one miserable piece at a time, and every now and then I get a hot lead or a glimpse of the big picture.

I've got my field notes in my trench coat, paying attention to things I've missed before. When Jasmine likes something, she rolls her eyes into the back of her head.

Rolled eyes at sushi *annotates*

Rolled eyes at everything bagel *annotates* *with lox and cream cheese* *annotates again and flip-closes notebook cover*

I'm paying attention to the things that she likes (and hates) because I'm in a relationship with Jasmine. The experts say that I'm supposed to find out what she likes and loves by doing the things she likes. But that's hard because (instinctually) I want to love her the way that I want to be loved, and some of her preferences make absolutely no sense to me.

Take the case of avocado toast, for instance.

Jasmine is Australian, and Australians are obsessed with avocado toast. They'll pay $26 for avocado toast, which is an entree, a main event, on their menus. It's insanity. I'm a Canadian—in Canada, toast is essentially garbage. In Canada, you go to a grungy diner for breakfast, not some hoity-toity yuppie café. And us Canadians order the "Big Breakfast"—eggs, bacon, sausage links, back bacon, mushrooms, maybe some beans—and you eat all that good stuff and then you wipe your face with the toast and throw it on the ground because toast is trash. Or, if for some horrible reason you're still hungry and you've run out of food to eat, you begrudgingly put jam from the little packets on the toast (in order to mask the taste of toast) and eat it reluctantly.

I would never think of loving my wife by giving her avocado toast for breakfast.

But that is what Jasmine loves, and I love Jasmine, and I want to show her that I see her and hear her and watch her: I want to show her that I'm present in our relationship and that my heart is in this thing that we have. And so I'm paying attention and learning things I didn't know about avocado toast.

It's not just regular toast that she likes—she likes sourdough toast—and thick cut, if they have it. When I make a Trader Joe's run, I go get the right loaf. And I've learned how to pick an avocado. If I press my thumb into it too far, it's too ripe; if my thumb doesn't go in when I press, it's not ripe at all. It's gotta be just right. And we have to have the best olive oil to drizzle over the top—it's gotta be a high-quality producer Italian brand and in a tiny cute bottle, not some huge store-brand bottle with no panache. And the salt has to be the fancy kind that you grind up, not cheap table salt.

I'm paying attention to her preferences. I may not understand them, but I don't need to. I have to overcome the reality that people have preferences and we shouldn't begrudge them their personal preferences.

God is a Person.[2]

He has preferences.

The Scriptures are God's self-revelation. In them, He has revealed Himself—and His preferences.

I can't know Jasmine accurately unless Jasmine reveals herself—anything else would just be projection. In order for me to know Jasmine, I gotta shut my mouth and let her speak. And I gotta listen and pay attention. From what she says and from what she does I can form images of who she is. But if I just tell her who she is and what she likes and doesn't like, I don't know Jasmine. I know nothing but a projected fantasy.

The Scriptures tell us from the very start that God is a Person. Genesis 1:26–27 tells us that God created human-ity in His image. We are people with a mind and will and

---

2. God is not a vibe. He's not the Universe. He's a Person. For more on God being a Per-son, particularly three persons yet One God (the Trinity), see Wayne Gruden, *Systematic Theology: An Introduction to Bible Doctrine, Second Edition* (Grand Rapids: Zondervan Academic), 269–82.

intellect and emotions, and God has a mind (1 Cor. 2:11) and a will (1 Cor. 1:1) and an intellect (Ps. 139:17) and emotions (Ps. 78:41). And this is all so much more on display in the Incarnation of the Second Person of the Trinity, Jesus Christ.[3]

And the plot thickens: Christians are in relationship with Him.

This is where that whole Religion vs. Relationship debate starts to get interesting, because there's a lot of Christians out there who don't seem to understand how a relationship works. They know religion alright—which is usually characterized by order, duty, rules, regulations, etc.—but they don't seem to understand relationship.

Relationships that work certainly have order, duty, rules, and regulations; there are certain things you cannot do in a marriage, if you want it to last. Marriage has routines, it has a rhythm; successful marriages are filled with order and boundaries and respect and honor.

Why is it that I continually get the impression when a Christian says, "It's not a religion, it's a relationship," it connotes they can do whatever they want, they are unaccountable to anyone except themselves, and that Jesus is buckled up in the back seat of their car while they are up front, deciding where everything goes. I imagine Jesus is in the back seat, freaked out because Todd's driving is

---

3. During His time on earth, Jesus had a personality, wept, grieved, experienced anxiety in the garden where He sweat drops of blood, exhibited joy and gladness and sorrow and friendship and all the things that make one a person. The Holy Spirit is not an "it" as many Charismatics mistakenly call Him, but rather a Person who can be grieved; He has a mind and a will; the Father has a mind and will and shows displeasure or pleasure. God is Spirit and yet possesses a corporality that is repeatedly seen and reported in Scripture, a substance that is unique from time, space, and matter—a substance in a category all by itself, or rather, Himself. On God's emotions, see Herman Bavnick, *The Doctrine of God*, trans. and ed. William Hendrickson (Grand Rapids: Eerdmans, 1951), 86–89.

reckless, and He's interceding in desperation.

"Buckle up, Lord—we're doing whatever I wanna do tonight [squawks tires]!"

Dude, marriage is hard; it's work! It requires perpetual selflessness and repentance, a constant laying down of one's desires and preferences, and a picking up and paying attention to the other's preferences.

A relationship doesn't mean that you get to do what you want—no way! A relationship is so much harder than a religion. A religion is easy—you can mail that in all day. Not a relationship!

Yes—we are in a relationship with God. And that means finding out what He likes and what He doesn't like, and doing what He likes.

Christian worship is giving God the avocado toast.

You don't need to understand God's preferences or why He likes certain things and not others; you just need to know what they are and do them—if you wanna be in a relationship with God.

Now, it is absolutely worth being in a relationship with God because you are the beneficiary of that relationship. God gets nothing out of being in relationship with us—we don't add to His life at all. He is perfectly satisfied in a triune relationship and needs nothing. He delights in us, and loves us, and rejoices over us, but He doesn't get anything or need anything from us. In fact, quite the opposite—it costs God everything to love us. The Second Person of the Trinity was tortured and murdered for us, in fact. God's heart is regularly wounded by us; He is grieved and experiences sorrow because of us. It was not safe for

Jesus to love us, but He loved us anyway.

No, we are the ones who get the better end of the deal in this relationship with God.

WORSHIP AS A PRIMARY MISSION

The primary mission of the church is to worship God first and foremost. It's not justice, it's not education, it's not to evangelize, it's not to equip the saints, it's not to Influence the world—all these things are certainly part of the mission of the church, but they are not the first and primary mission of the church. This is where things have gone sideways for so many Christians and what continues to cause so much confusion around the church and its relationship to God.

The Westminster Catechism reads:

What is the chief end of man?
The chief end of man is to glorify God and enjoy Him forever.[4]

As in, *Why do I exist as a human?* I exist in relationship to God to worship God. That is my primary purpose in life, and everything else flows from that. The first proof from Scripture given to support this statement is Psalm 86:9: "All the nations you have made shall come and worship before you, O Lord, and shall glorify your name."

In this same vein, the primary purpose of the

4. Westminster Assembly, Douglas F. Kelly, Philip B. Rollinson, and Fredrick T. Marsh, *The Westminster Shorter Catechism in Modern English* (Phillipsburg, NJ: Presbyterian and Reformed Pub. Co. 1986), 1.

church—in accordance with the primary purpose of humanity—is to worship God.

Old Testament scholar Daniel Block says that defining worship in the Bible is difficult, but the phenomena can be described as "reverential human acts of submission and homage before the divine Sovereign in response to his gracious revelation of himself and in accord with his will."[5]

Following Block's description, worship in the Bible involves reverent awe (Heb. 12:28)—this was seen through the cultic preparations of the temple and priesthood. Though equipping the saints and justice are both important aspects of worship, they are secondary to the primary expression: our reverence before God Himself as we minister to Him in the place of His choosing in the modes and methods that He prefers.

Next, we see worship in the Bible as a human response. The Psalter primarily speaks of worship as directed to YHWH Himself; it certainly talks of doing justice and reaching the nations and the process of discipleship, but its loudest tone is a call for everything that has breath to praise YHWH—to express thankfulness for His goodness through "blessing His name"—a ministry of words and hands and knees and feet and thoughts and gifts and sacrifices to YHWH.

God set Israel—the first church in the wilderness— free to worship Him, to establish the cultic rituals and practices of YHWH worship as revealed by YHWH to

---

5. Daniel I. Block, *For the Glory of God: Recovering a Biblical Theology of Worship* (Grand Rapids: Baker Academic, 2016), 23.

Moses (Exod. 7:16). Martha was busy doing all the work, while Mary sat at the feet of Jesus who chose the better thing (Luke 10:38–42). In John 12:1–7, John absolutely rips critics of worship by showing us it was Judas Iscariot who bristled at Mary's extravagant worship when she wasted a year's wages on Jesus's feet, saying that the money could've gone to the poor. Worship is never too extravagant for Jesus and never wasted—it takes precedent over everything else that we do.

Wayne Grudem writes, "Worship in the church is not merely a preparation for something else: it is in itself fulfilling the major purpose of the church with reference to its Lord."[6]

The church cannot lose laser focus of its primary reason for existence. Perhaps in our desire to reach more people or better our public relations or improve our ability to disciple, we have lost our *raison d'être*.

It's interesting that the church in Ephesus—the church to which Paul writes the most revelatory doctrine on the genesis and purpose and eternal vision of the church—is the one that Jesus says, "Hey, you've lost your first love and you need to get it back."[7] There's a warning in the next several verses: retrace your steps and get back to primary purposes, or else you won't be a church anymore.

Later in Revelation 5, God worship is set on display. John is saying, "This is what worship looks like. This is why we were created—worship God!"

Worship as a primary focus of the church is God's preference.

---

6. Gruden, *Systematic Theology*, 1064.
7. See Revelation 2:4.

THE STRATEGY

God also has a preferential strategy for the church because He knows how to build it and what its purposes are.

Last week my brother-in-law and I started playing Pickle Ball. Everyone in "the desert" (area of Palm Springs, California) seems to be obsessed with Pickle Ball, and so we wanted in.

We bought paddles, balls, and season passes to a tennis club where nobody plays tennis and everyone plays Pickle Ball.

I don't have much of a tennis past but I've played Ping-Pong (don't judge) for most of my life. I know how to put nasty spin on the ball, crush a forehand shot, and drop shots that are incapable of retrieval. We played about four times in one week and I was starting to get pretty cocky; my forehands were getting more dialed in, I was hitting the ball harder and harder—it was all coming together rather nicely.

On Friday, we were playing beside two ladies in their early sixties. I was watching their lobbies back and forth and snickering to myself, "Wow, they suck." They were doing these seemingly simple drills at the front of the net, back and forth, without any power or creativity. I'm thinking, *I'm gonna dominate this Pickle Ball Club. These old goats will be buying me rounds of Pedialyte for days.*

Just before we were about to leave, the GM of the club came up and asked us if we wanted to play a doubles match against the antiques beside us. I rolled my eyes and thought, *Don't smash any shots and rock the boat, go easy*.

"Sure, we'd love to."

The ladies agreed also and we were off.

What transpired for the next hour was a humiliation of biblical proportions.

We watched these ladies trounce us seven games in a row. We landed maybe four points in the entire seven of the eleven-point games!

We were better strikers, more athletic, quicker to drop shots, and had faster serves, but they played a strategic game between them that absolutely destroyed us.

I didn't know the strategy of the game, and thought I could rely on my individual ability to better our opponents. I was totally mistaken.

Every generation has its critiques and fresh expressions of the church—from the Rococo movement in the Catholic Church to the Charismatic movement in Evangelicalism. Making Christianity culturally approachable and accessible by the natives is paramount. Martin Luther, William Booth, and the Wesley brothers used to take popular folk songs and simply change the lyrics. *Voilà*—you've instantly got everyone singing because they know the tune.

I love the enculturation and beautification process of the gospel.

But there seems to be other things going on of late with respect to the church, and it's an attempt to change more than the color of the carpet in the sanctuary.

I chalk it up to a radical individualism[8] that rejects both biblical and historic strategy in favor of modern hunches and expressions. It's a disregard for God's preferred strategy and an overestimation of modern ingenuity.

There are also some flawed premises: my generation falsely thinks the church has failed, is failing, and we need to totally "rethink" church. There's no doubt the church has its problems and growth points, both currently and historically. But these suggest that core doctrines need to be revisited and changed. That the focus needs to be activism and philanthropy. The table needs to be "lengthened" to include historically "marginalized" groups (people who reject biblical definitions of sin or core doctrines such as repentance, hell, etc.). Buildings should be sold and emphases on in-person gatherings should be traded for a kind of Gnostic,[9] disembodied spirituality straight out of a dystopian future novel.

But God has a purpose, plan, and preferred strategy for the church.

And He's revealed it in Scripture.

It's not super complex, but it works.

Here's some stuff to consider as we work that out:

First, God does the saving (Eph. 2:5; 2 Tim. 1:9). I don't save people, the Holy Spirit does. Yes, I proclaim the

---

8. According to Yuval Levin, individualism is "not only a desire to pursue one's own path but also a yearning for fulfillment through the definition and articulation of one's own identity. It is a drive both to be more like whatever you already are and also to live in society by fully asserting who you are. The capacity of individuals to define the terms of their own existence by defining their personal identities is increasingly equated with liberty and with the meaning of some of our basic rights, and it is given pride of place in our self-understanding." See Yuval Levin, *The Fractured Republic: Renewing America's Social Contract in the Age of Individualism* (New York: Basic Books, 2017), 148.

9. For a thorough look at Gnosticism, including its origins and practices, see Kurt Rudolph, "Gnosticism" in David Noel Freedman (ed.), *Anchor Bible Dictionary* (New York: Doubleday, 1992), 1033–40.

gospel, but the Spirit does the work of conversion.

Second, God does the adding—when God is saving someone, He adds them to the church (Acts 2:47). God saves, God adds. Or as Paul says, God gives the increase and growth (1 Cor. 3:6). Yes, I do the work of creating welcoming and discipling atmospheres, but God is saving, and the church is where He puts people whom He loves.

Why does God adds to the church when He saves? Because He is a Father, and fathers understand the importance of family. Psalm 68:6 (NIV) reads, "God sets the lonely in families." When we are Spirit-born, we desire the "pure milk of the word" (1 Pet. 2:2 NKJV). I can always tell that the Holy Spirit is doing a regenerating work in a person, because they will have a voracious appetite for the things of God—babies eat. And we receive the "pure milk of the word" in the local church (Acts 2:42), where believers "continue in the apostles' teaching." We need feeders. That's what shepherds are and that's where they receive their authority to lead a church—from their Christ-gift ability to feed.

If you can't feed, you shouldn't lead, because God's plan for the church is not for a social club led by a guy who knows business—that is not playing into the preferred plan of God as blueprinted in Scripture.

"Well, Nate, the thief on the cross never went to church or learned Bible teaching . . ."

True, but we don't build doctrine from the thief on the cross; we temper it. So it is possible to be a Christian and not go to church or grow in our knowledge of God, but it is not probable, because if you aren't nailed to a cross and will live for longer than fifteen seconds, God's requirements of you and purposes for you will be radically different.

For example, the thief on the cross wasn't baptized. Does that mean we should disobey Jesus's *command* to be baptized (Acts 10:48)? No, but there will obviously be people who die before they can obey that command. If baptism were the only way to be saved, the thief on the cross wouldn't have gone to paradise.

Third, God's preferred strategy for the local church is physical proximal togetherness. Notice the "togethers" in this description of the very first church in Acts 2:42–47:

> And they devoted themselves to the apostles' teaching and the fellowship, to the breaking of bread and the prayers. And awe came upon every soul, and many wonders and signs were done through the apostles. And all who believed were *together* and had all things in common. And they were selling their possessions and belongings and distributing the proceeds to all, as any had need. And day by day, attending the temple *together* and breaking bread in their homes, they received their food with glad and generous hearts, praising God and having favor with all the people. And the Lord added to their number day by day those who were being saved.

Going to a local church and being fully integrated into the daily physical life of the church is God's plan for every believer.

In Romans 12:1–2, Paul argues that the most logical response of worship to God's plan of salvation is that believers present their bodies as a living sacrifice as an acceptable form of worship. Immediately after, in verse 5, Paul claims that believers are members who belong to one another.

You belong to me, and I belong to you, and without you I am incomplete, and without me you are incomplete. I need your physical presence in the church, and you need mine. I need you to show up and be present, and you need me to show up and be present. When you and I show up in physical proximal togetherness for the purpose of exalting Jesus, the Holy Spirit shows up, who mediates the Presence of Jesus. When the Spirit shows up, we begin to encourage one another by the Spirit. I need your prophetic exhortation and you need mine, because that's how the church builds itself up in love (1 Cor. 14:1–5). We all, no matter our gifts, are enabled by the Holy Spirit to encourage and exhort one another!

This is God's plan. And if we follow God's plan, God will do the work of saving and adding to the church, and the church will grow numerically and in spiritual strength as it devotes itself to praising God, the apostles' teaching, and the fellowship of Christ.

From this momentum and strength, the church moves into mission.

Loving God His way, seeing the church God's way,

and then experiencing fully embodied participation in the life of the church God's way is how we demonstrate to the Lord that we are in a relationship with Him on His terms, ever so conscious of His preferences. This is worship.

Chapter Two

YOU'RE A PRIEST

In Psalm 141 we find David writing a "Band-on-the-Run" psalm—he's away from the tabernacle for some reason, perhaps because he's on the run from Absalom, his son, who was staging a coup.

David was obsessed with the tabernacle; he loved the Presence of God.

But he couldn't be near the tabernacle because he was stuck out in the wilderness, avoiding being assassinated. So he begins to pen this "I Miss Your Presence" song to God, and it goes like this:

"Let my prayer be counted as incense before you . . ."

David is praying through the tabernacle furniture here, because he's intimately familiar with the layout of God's House.

In the tabernacle there was the Holy of Holies, where the ark of the covenant,[10] the literal throne of God on

10. The ark of the covenant, you know—that golden box from Indiana Jones where they open it at the end of *Raiders of the Lost Ark* and it melts the Nazi's face off? Yeah, that one. See Marten H. Woudstra, "Ark of the Covenant" in Walter A. Elwell (ed.), *Baker Encyclopedia of the Bible* (Grand Rapids: Baker Book House, 1988), 169–72.

earth, was placed. No one was allowed to casually just hang out in there. It was God's green room. Only priests of the highest order on the right occasions were able to go in there. And there was this thick veil that separated the Holy of Holies from the Holy Place, which was God's "court" so to speak, where the rest of the sacred furniture for various duties and offerings was kept. Immediately outside the Holy of Holies—on the other side of the veil—was this table with a bowl of incense. This was the closest piece of furniture to the ark—the incense was so close that God could smell it on the other side of the curtain. And the priests were to keep that incense burning perpetually—morning and evening—for all times.

So in Psalm 141:2, David is saying, "God, I know I'm way far away from You in the wilderness, but I need Your help right now and I'm asking that my prayer to You from far away would be like that incense right outside Your green room—that incense so close You can smell it. And that it would be a pleasing aroma that would get Your attention."

David is writing all this by the Spirit[11] and is prophetically describing the prayers of the saints, as we see in the book of Revelation.[12] And David is bang on: the prayers of the righteous (those who have been brought close by

---

11. Jesus affirms that David writes under the inspiration of the Spirit in Matthew 22:43. R. T. France confirms this: "And when David used that term [Lord] he was *inspired by the Spirit* (literally just 'in [the] Spirit'), i.e., he spoke as a prophet." See R. T. France, *Matthew: An Introduction and Commentary* (Downers Grove, IL: IVP Press, 1985), 325 (first bracket mine).

12. See Revelation 5:8; 6:9–11; 8:4–5. In Revelation, we see multiple prayer bowls before the throne of God that are the prayers of the saints. Prayer is such an important theme in Revelation that G. K. Beale and David Campbell offer a suggested reflection on Revelation 8:1–5 that comments on "the effectiveness of prayer." See G. K. Beale and David Campbell, *Revelation: A Shorter Commentary* (Grand Rapids: Eerdmans, 2015), 168.

the blood of Jesus) reach the throne of God. We have that type of proximity wherever we are.

Then he says, "And the lifting up of my hands as the evening sacrifice!"

When we think of the biblical authors, particularly the Old Testament authors, we have to remember they are acutely aware of Torah (the first five books of the Old Testament); or to put it another way, Genesis to Deuteronomy is their Bible. It's the only way they know about God. They don't know YHWH outside of Torah, and cannot, in the same way that you and I don't know God outside of the Scriptures and the revelation of Jesus Christ.

YHWH revealed Himself to Moses in a similar way that Jesus revealed Himself to the disciples (Num. 12:8).

David knew about YHWH from Torah, and he writes songs about God as if he's singing the book of Deuteronomy ("the book of grace") aloud.

David knows what YHWH loves—he's read Torah.

David wants to please YHWH—he desires YHWH's Presence.

So when David says, "Let the lifting up of my hands be like the evening sacrifice," he's saying, "YHWH—I love You and have experienced Your Presence and I'm committed to You. I know what You like—I've read what Your preferences are in worship. You have asked for specific sacrifices, and I want to show You that I'm in this relationship. I want to give You the avocado toast. I want to give You the things that delight Your heart. But I cannot appear before You at the tabernacle, the resting place of Your glory where the ark is. But I want to please You right now where I am, here in the wilderness. And I need Your Presence right now. Would the lifting of my hands be like the evening sacrifices that bless Your heart?"

Once again, David is praying this prophetically by the Spirit. And he is right.

God loves hands.

The Hebrew word for hand is *yad*.[13] One of the main Hebrew words for praise is *yadah*. It literally means "to wave the hand." In the Hebrew mind, praise involves hands. Especially now that David—led by the Spirit—has established a worship precedent with respect to the lifting of hands.

What does this all mean?

God loves lifted hands to Him. They please His heart. He has revealed this about Himself in Scripture. And as someone who is in relationship with Him, I want to know His preferences as revealed in Scripture so that I can give Him what He wants.

THE PLOT THICKENS

Fast-forward to the New Testament era.

The author of the book of Hebrews is writing to a bunch of Christian Jews scattered throughout the Mediterranean who are struggling with their faith: they are thinking about leaving Jesus because of how rough the persecution is.

They are also facing scrutiny by Jews who are picking their newfound faith apart.

---

13. See *Eerdmans Dictionary of the Bible*, ed. David Noel Freedman (Grand Rapids: Eerdmans, 2000), 388.

Their detractors are saying, "Christianity is lame: you don't have a priesthood or a temple, so you can't bring sacrifices to God; the Law was revealed to Moses, how can you possibly compare Jesus to Moses? Also, you are the children of Israel with a rich heritage of faith: why would you leave the people who were delivered from Egypt by YHWH?"

These are some serious critiques. The Hebrew Christians are panicking. So the author of Hebrews is going to write a polemic against these issues being raised and establish some really great doctrine for the church.

He starts by telling the Hebrews that Jesus is better than Moses. "Better" is a theme throughout Hebrews. We could even call Hebrews the "Better Book."[14]

Jesus is better than Moses because He's God.

The New Covenant is a better covenant because it removes sins.

People who hear and have faith in Jesus are better than those who die in the wilderness of unbelief.[15]

Jesus's priesthood is a better priesthood because it's eternal and He doesn't die.

We can offer better sacrifices as New Testament believers because we offer them *through* Jesus and *to* Jesus, who is a better Priest.

In Hebrews 13, the author is wrapping up and he's giving practical instructions on worship so that these Hebrew Christians feel like their worship is real. Keeping

---

14. Donald Guthrie notes that the writer of Hebrews' "line of approach was that everything in fact was better—a better sanctuary, a better priesthood, a better sacrifice, a better covenant." See Donald Guthrie, *Hebrews: An Introduction and Commentary* (Grand Rapids: Wm. B. Eerdmans, 1983), 32–33.
15. See Hebrews 3:17.

in mind that the Old Testament is their Bible (which they are intimately acquainted with), the author will copy and paste Psalm 141:2 and give it some new meaning.

This is important because Old Testament precedent (biblical precedent) is important for these Christians. If they can see it in their Bibles, they will be stirred up in the knowledge that they are still obeying YHWH and showing covenant loyalty and faith to YHWH, and they can see the continuity between YHWH and Jesus.

Hebrews 13:15 (NIV) reads, "Through Jesus, therefore, let us continually offer to God a sacrifice of praise—the fruit of lips that openly profess his name."

The original audience would know exactly where the author is pulling this idea from: Psalm 141![16]

David—easily a Hebrew favorite—establishes precedent for YHWH worship that is outside of the temple. We see prayers and lifted hands that are close to YHWH and are like the evening sacrifice.

The New Testament church can run with this idea!

Then the author of Hebrews will give more instructions on sacrifice in the very next verse: "And do not forget to do good and to share with others, for with such sacrifices God is pleased" (NIV).

So the Hebrews can offer sacrifices and worship through Jesus—and these other sacrifices are all found in Torah as well, like who should share in the long distance

---

16. I am taking Hebrews 13:15 to be an allusion to Psalm 141. Beale defines an "allusion" as a "brief expression consciously intended by an author to be dependent on an OT passage. In contrast to a quotation of the OT, which is a direct reference, allusions are indirect references (the OT wording is not reproduced directly as in a quotation)." Beale also notes there are anywhere from 600 to 4,100 of these in the NT. See G. K. Beale, *Handbook on the New Testament Use of the Old Testament* (Grand Rapids: Baker Academic, 2012), 31.

tithe, or instructions on reaping the wheat harvest and gathering the grapes, or instructions on how to treat the widow, orphan, foreigner, and poor.

SACRIFICES

The word "sacrifice" doesn't seem to fit into the theological landscape of your average Charismatic Evangelical, because we seem to have a fundamental lack of clarity on what grace means.

Grace doesn't mean that you don't have to do anything.

Grace isn't opposed to works; it's opposed to merit.

It means that you don't deserve to be saved and can do nothing to deserve to be saved, because your righteousness is about as good as a pile of dirty underwear.

You are saved by grace through faith, not by works. You can't boast about being saved by grace because it had nothing to do with your best efforts.

But grace empowers and fuels works: there's more to grace than mercy. Mercy is one significant part of grace, but it's not the whole story. Mercy covers, grace empowers.

And we need to take into account that the New Testament is constantly telling Christians to "sacrifice" and give "sacrifices" that please God.

So then we can say that I am saved by grace, not by works, but that I am called to "lay hold of that for which Christ Jesus has also laid hold of me" (Phil. 3:12 NKJV). As in, there's work to do, and the grace of God will empower me for every good work in Christ Jesus.

And we also say that I do not sacrifice for the forgive-ness of sins—which is where so many Christians lose their understanding of this word and concept.

Jesus died 2,000 years ago and took all of the sins of the world upon Himself. Jesus dealt with sin once and for all, for all those who believe in Him and apply the blood of His once-and-for-all, unrepeatable sacrifice for sins to their life by faith.

I don't sacrifice for the forgiveness of sins, I sacrifice *from* the forgiveness of sins, because I get to be in a rela-tionship with God because of Jesus.

This is what Paul means when he writes to the Romans, "Therefore, I urge you, brothers and sisters, in view of God's mercy [in light of everything that God has done through the cross!], to offer your bodies as a living sacrifice" (12:1 NIV).

Jesus paid it all, all to Him I owe—as the old song goes.[17]

So I'm not trying to "do good and share what I have" or "continually offer a sacrifice of praise to God" as some sort of ablution. I'm forgiven, and now I have a reason for living—a holy calling to which I'm called—and that holy calling involves sacrifices.

I'm a priest.

First Peter 2:5 (NIV) reads, "You also, like living stones, are being built into a spiritual house to be a holy priest-hood, offering spiritual sacrifices acceptable to God through Jesus Christ."

This verse was foundational to the Protestant

---

17. Elvina M. Hall, "Jesus Paid It All," 1865, Public Domain.

Reformation. This was one of Martin Luther's 95 problems with the Catholic Church. When Luther read this, it jumped off the pages of holy writ like a spooked frog.[18]

I don't need a priest; I am a priest!

In fact, every believer is a priest!

But there is a weight to this idea that seems to have been lost in many of our churches. The responsibility of a Protestant church is that every believer functions as a priest: they all give, they all worship, they all share, they all contribute to the vitality of the church—every joint supplies.

And when this doesn't happen, the mass model actually becomes more appealing. A passive historical church experience in which everything is done by the clergy is a better experience than a consumeristic congregation gawking at the stage like a tree full of owls.

Protestant churches are designed for participatory experiences. They cannot sustain consumerism, and neither can Protestant Christians who become consumers rather than priests. Their faith won't survive that transition.

I'm convinced that the weight of Protestantism is too great for Western Protestants, who have forgotten the responsibility of the priesthood for the respite of passive consumerism.

I'm also convinced that Deconstruction[19] is the product of a Christianity that produces congregants whose spirituality is dwarfed "for lack of exercise" and need the

---

18. Luther says, "It is pure invention that pope, bishops, priests and monks are to be called the 'spiritual estate'; princes lords, artisans, and farmers the 'temporal estate' . . . all Christians are truly of the 'spiritual estate,' and there is among them no difference at all but that of office." See Martin Luther, "To the Christian Nobility of the German Nation" in *Luther's Works*, 44:129.

19. Brian Zahnd describes Deconstruction as "a crisis of Christian faith that leads to either reevaluation of Christianity or sometimes a total abandonment of Christianity." See Brian Zahnd, *When Everything's on Fire: Faith Forged from the Ashes* (Downers Grove, IL: IVP Press, 2021), 26.

foundational principles again. There is no root because there has been no function. Christianity is not a head game, it's holistic. The way you learn Christ matters. A passive cerebral experience does not create disciples, and coupled with the continual existential crisis that is post-modernism, it only creates a Mars Hill of Christian philosophers who don't know Christ or His power.

We have churches full of detached Gnostic consumers: they don't think their body and its work is integral to their spirituality, which causes their relationship to church to depend on whether or not it serves them. They are more concerned about what their church can do for them than what they can do for their church.

Consumerism is killing the Western Protestant church.

Everywhere else a Christian goes, she is a Consumer.

She votes with her dollars (yay free market capitalism) and seeks out business transactions that make her feel important and valued. Now I have no problem with that: you should never go to a restaurant that makes you feel unwelcome and serves you cold food. I love free market capitalism because it rewards good business and punishes bad business.

But getting back to my point—we are immersed in the world of beneficial transaction all day long.

Our steps are determined by what suits us.

- Is it close by? How far is it? I can't be bothered to go that far.
- Is it busy? How busy? I have so much to do, my time is so important.

- Is it cheap? How cheap? Bargains make me feel powerful.
- Do you get a lot? How much do you get? I need to feel pampered like Cleopatra.
- Does it look nice? How nice? I need to feel like James Dean walking in that joint.
- Does it make me feel cool? I gotta be cool. I'll just die if it's cringe. I'm a 4 Wing 5.
- Is it luxurious? I only associate with luxury brands. I'm so important and demand respect.
- Do the staff make a big fuss about my every whim? I need things just right. It's about me.

This type of thinking is so engrained in our advertising and consuming—and these patterns of thinking are so habitual and daily rehearsed—that it's almost impossible to get out of.

We even have apps that help us reward and destroy businesses based on our experiences and preferences.

One of my favorite episodes of *South Park* is the one where Kyle's dad becomes a Yelp reviewer. He secretly stays up into the wee small hours of the morning, typing feverishly on the family computer, writing one lengthy consumer review after another. He's a caricature of your average consumer, obsessed with the process of adjudication. There is something in it that makes us feel powerful and important.

It's not really shocking, then, that Christians who habitually practice consumerism—the holy hourly liturgy of secularism—bring this posture into the church, creating an audience rather than a church.

When I come to church, I'm not a consumer—as Peter notes—I'm a priest.

Peter says, "You, like living stones, are being built into a spiritual house . . ."

I'm not alone in this salvation of mine—God has designed me as a building block. This is a first principle that is so important to underline again: *I belong to the spiritual house because I'm a living stone.*

I'm a rolling stone on the couch in my underwear on a Sunday morning while I groggily eat cereal and stream church online. I'm a living stone when I physically show up to church with my big boy pants on. At home I am living a detached spirituality where I see myself as getting something, whereas at church I am living an embodied spirituality where I participate in the life of the church, giving and partaking of the Presence of Christ unique to the gathering of the believers.

I was made to be a part. I'm a living stone.

I was made to build a church. I am a living stone.

Peter continues, ". . . being built into a spiritual house, to be a holy priesthood . . ."

I am a priest. I have received a priesthood. This must be my posture as a believer.

And that priesthood is accomplished in the structure of the spiritual house, as Peter is suggesting here in context. I'm not a priest in my underwear at home; I'm a priest in church with the gathering of the saints, who gather to worship God and minister to one another.

What do priests do? Priests minister to the Lord and others, in that order.

My primary job as a priest is to minister to the Lord, my secondary job as a priest is to minister to the saints and the world.

And how do I do that?

With the sacrifices.

Peter continues, ". . . to be a holy priesthood, offering spiritual sacrifices acceptable to God through Jesus Christ."

So when I come to church, I'm on duty. I'm not there for me; I'm there for the Lord and His people.

I'm not at church to Yelp review the sound, the lights, the chairs, the carpet, whether or not the cross is visible, the pastor's clothes, the song selection, and how useful for my spiritual journey the message was.

Church is not about me; it's about Him and His.

I am a priest, and I've brought sacrifices.

When I was a kid, we used to sing this song in church, "We bring the sacrifice of praise into the House of the Lord. And we offer up to you the sacrifices of thanksgiving . . ."[20]

It had this awful cringe music and the melody was a crime against humanity—it was honestly a horrible piece of art, even for its time. But the theology was just so good. We were singing about what we were doing. We knew our jobs. And we brought it.

We were saying, "God, I'm here for You! And I've

---

20. Kirk Dearman, "We Bring the Sacrifice of Praise," Brentwood-Benson Music Publishing, Inc., 1984.

brought what You like. You like hands lifted to You and clapped to You in worship, and so here are mine. I love You, and this is my holy service to You. And You want us to come before You with thanksgiving in our hearts, and so we are singing songs of thanksgiving and joy. We are thankful for what You have done for us."

That church was amazing. It was a church full of priests. Churches with priests are biblically demonstrative churches. They don't do things because they feel like it or because they fit culturally, as if worship is some bad form of karaoke. Churches filled with priests are loud, hand lifting, participatory churches that bring "acceptable sacrifices," as Peter specifically details.

Acceptable sacrifices are sacrifices that God has asked for.

Priests are careful to minister to the Lord the way that He has asked. They do not presume, assume, or speculate upon worship that pleases the Lord. Rather, they give Him exactly what He has required.

To assume, presume, and speculate upon worship is to place oneself stubbornly in a seat of power, as if one's preferences were to be preferred over the other's preferences. Worshipping God how we want instead of how God wants may be one of the most ignorant and arrogant things we could do.

"Well, I worship God in my heart." That's not how relationships work, as we established earlier. And you don't just have a relationship with God; you are a priest. You have a job to do: the priesthood is literally your job.

This isn't Old Testament teaching; this is New

Testament. We've read Romans, 1 Peter, and Hebrews so far. Paul brings up sacrifices two other times, and one of them is financial. Do a Greek word study on *thysia* in the New Testament.[21] You won't be able to avoid the New Covenant reality of spiritual sacrifices.

See, what makes us uncomfortable about all this is our disposition toward a Gnostic spirituality. What I mean by Gnostic is the Neo-Platonic idea that matter is bad and spirit is good, thus God really doesn't care so much about matter and presentness and obedience as much as He cares about my internal worship. But as we read the entirety of Scriptures, we see worship as something that is believed and lived; it involves hearts and hands. And it is conscious of the Divine Sovereign's requirements and preferences.

The church must recover the spiritual reality of the priesthood, that is, a church that gathers to give to the Lord the worship that is due His name, in His way.

The church must reject forms of spirituality that stunt the growth of the believer. It is in *doing* that we grow in our walk with Jesus because our walk is more than just believing.

And the doing has to be seen as a work of grace, not a work for grace. We must see our priesthood as Aaron was told to see it, as a gift (Num. 18:7), and the ability to approach God as an incredible privilege, not something to be borne.

We need to completely re-evaluate our posture as it pertains to church gatherings. We are not there to get; we

---

21. See Johannes Behm, "θύω, θυσία, θυσιαστήριον" in Gerhard Kittel, Geoffrey W. Bromiley, and Gerhard Friedrich (eds.), *Theological Dictionary of the New Testament* (Grand Rapids: Eerdmans, 1964), 180–90.

are there to give. And paradoxically, those who refresh others will themselves be refreshed, as we observed earlier. I'm at church to minister to the Lord. I have appeared before Him for that reason primarily. We must reject consumerism as our modus operandi and recover the fires of Protestantism if we are to be a church on fire.

Chapter Three

TURN YOUR AMP UP TO 11

I'll never forget where I was when I read Psalm 57 for the first time.

I was a junior in Bible college and I was in Dorm 3—the all-boys dormitory of Portland Bible College in Portland, Oregon. My dorm leader at the time was my friend Lance McGinnis from Salt Lake City, Utah.

Lance came up to me "like a bridegroom coming out of his chamber," with the excitement that only Lance possessed on campus. Quite randomly he exclaimed, "Did you know that we have a glory?"

I'm like, "What?"

"Yeah dude—we have a glory. Check out this verse."

He proceeded to read Psalm 57:7–8 for me: "My heart is steadfast, O God, my heart is steadfast! I will sing and make melody. Awake, my glory! Awake, O harp and lyre! I will awake the dawn."

The passage was stuck in my spirit for fifteen years. I

didn't understand it and needed to chew on it. The timing wasn't right for me to study it. I socked it away for later.

Fast-forward fifteen years.

I was a teaching pastor at Hillsong NYC and was asked to teach at a church in Pennsylvania. For whatever reason I was reminded of this passage, so I sat down and went back through it. I got as excited as Lance did as I read and re-read.

The psalm is a "I'm in trouble, help me, God" song. David is "surrounded by lions"; he's feeling overwhelmed by the presence of his enemies and their constant plotting.

David begins to focus his soul on his strength—YHWH.

He is saying, "God, my heart is totally fixed on You. And I'm going to sing and play my guitar and focus my entire being on You."

And then he utters this powerful phrase, "Awake, my glory."

Usually the Bible talks about God's glory, so this is what threw me for a loop: Why would David talk about his own glory? Isn't that bad?

But David begins to define his glory: "Awake, my glory—awake, harp and lyre."

David's "glory" is his ability to make music.

It's his special power, his unique ability that distinguishes him from everyone else.

David was the Jimi Hendrix of the harp and lyre—he was bad to the bone. He was so good at playing the harp and lyre—so gifted and "gloried" by God at his craft—that troubling spirits would flee from people they were oppressing if they were within earshot of the music and corresponding atmosphere David would create (see 1 Sam. 16:23).

David's "glory" was music. He is arguably the greatest musical artist that ever lived. We still sing his songs as his discography has been canonized. He produced worship services (1 Chron. 15:16), he wrote songs, and he invented instruments (Amos 6:5).

In Psalm 57:7–8, David is saying, "God—I am going to turn my heart toward You because I so desperately need You. But I'm awakening the best part of me—my glory—I'm not mailing this thing in—I'm giving You my very best."

David straps on the Gibson Les Paul, plugs into a Marshall Stack, and turns it up to 11.

The big idea here is that humans have a glory. Now, all glory that humans have is on loan—or as philosophers might say—transcendent.[22] In the same way that all beauty is transcendent (in that it comes down from above) because God is the First and the Creator and thus all beauty flows from Him, the ultimately Beautiful One, all glory is transcendent—it comes from Him.

God gives humans glory. And part of our worship is returning glory. This is why the psalmist will say throughout the Psalms (like Psalm 29), "Give unto the LORD, O you mighty ones, Give unto the LORD glory and strength. Give unto the LORD the glory due to His name" (vv. 1–2 NKJV).

Worship is a return of glory—an incredibly self-conscious and humble act. This prerequisite of recognizing

---

22. For more on "transcendence," see John Lachs, "Transcendence in Philosophy and Everyday Life," *The Journal of Speculative Philosophy* 11, no. 4 (1997): 247–55.

from whom everything flows becomes fuel for worship.

David knows that all glory comes from God, and he needs God's glory, so he will stir up his glory.

The Hebrew word that we translate as "glory" here in English is *kabod*, and it literally means, "weight."[23] The idea behind "weight" is manifold: a primary use is what you're good at, what you bring to the table tangibly.

If I'm at a party and you walk into the room, I may lean over to the host and ask, "Who is that dude?" The host replies, "Oh that's so-and-so, and he's an amazing such-and-such, and he's a great golfer, and his business is amazing, he . . ."

That's your *kabod*. That's your weight.

It's why someone would call you on the phone and ask for help.

It's why someone would text you and request input on a project or some strategy about a situation.

It's a culmination of your interests, gifting, skills, time, lean, disposition, family proclivity, schooling, discipline—all of these precious things intersect at this glorious convergence point—the highest flower of your being, that we describe as your glory, your weight, your *kabod*.

Kabod isn't just what you're good at, it's also your present-ness, it's your dialed-in-ness, it's your spark.

I remember being at a staff Christmas party years ago in Manhattan. We were at some restaurant/club having a ball. We were young and alive in the Big Apple, church was growing, friends were plentiful around us, the food

---

23. Gregory R. Lanier, "Glory" in Douglas Magnum (ed.) et al., *Lexham Theological Workbook*, Lexham Bible Reference Series (Bellingham, WA: Lexham Press, 2014).

was delicious, and the music was bumping.

One of our staff—whom I would describe as an office-type—was at the party, chatting it up with friends and nursing one of those drinks with an umbrella in it. At this office, this individual was administrative—their *kabod* was organization, and Lord did we need them. They were the glue that bound us.

But here we were—a night out on the town—quite a different atmosphere, and almost everyone is dancing.

Now, as I suggested earlier, this person looked administrative, not like someone who dances. Administrative people have an adorable look to them, but it is not the look of someone who likes to dance.

All of a sudden, this person's song comes on. I think it was "You Make Me Wanna" by Usher, if my memory serves me correctly. They jumped up and started dancing. And it was the most awful and wonderful thing I had ever seen.

Have you ever been at a professional sports event where, during the commercial break or in between breaks of play, the DJ will start playing "YMCA" by The Village People and the cameras will start to pan in on some overweight, drunk-off-their-face fan with no shirt on, chest painted with team slogans, dancing with all their might and doing all the "YMCA" actions?

It's ugly yet beautiful; it's grotesque yet a sight to behold.

That's *kabod*.

There is something glorious in our present best effort, in our imperfect passion on full display.

Your *kabod* is what your wife falls in love with—it's that attention that you so freely lavished upon her on that first date. Remember? You were lost in her angelic face and attention as you stared at her while Steven Tyler was screeching in the background, ". . . and I don't wanna miss a thang . . ."

Present-ness is glory. It's intoxicating. It's power.

One of the ways I love my wife is by listening to her psychotic dreams.

She's one of those people that dreams every single night, and remembers them vividly. I'm not always eager to listen to her dreams because every now and then she'll tell me I was "mean to her at a party in my dream last night." Meanwhile, I was sleeping—quite innocently—beside her all through the night.

And I know she always loves to tell these stories about her dreams, so when we're out for a drive I'll ask her, "So—did you have any dreams last night?"

She lights up. "OMG, I was in Jurassic Park and I was being chased by a velociraptor . . ."

[makes eye contact, shows interest] "Really? What happened next?"

"Then a T-Rex came out of nowhere and started to attack the velociraptor . . ."

[stares at road, eyes glazed over] "Uh-huh. Yep. Yuh. Uh-huh."

Without fail, my wife will catch me drifting and snap her fingers, "Nathan—where are you?"

And God is like a woman. He knows when you're not there.

What does all of this mean?

See, God wants hands (Hebrew, *yad*), but He also wants glory (Hebrew, *kabod*).

God wants *yad* and *kabod*.

Yes, find out His preferences of worship and give those to Him; give Him the avocado toast.

But He also wants a life behind that offering.

It's so easier for all of us to offer worship that is detached from our glory.

I'm the most ADD worshipper ever. One minute I'm passionately singing "Amazing Grace" with my hands raised in adoration, and the next minute I'm wondering when Tom Brady will retire from football.

God wants more than just my hands; He wants my glory—my best, my attention, my power.

And there seems to be a divorce between our *yad* and *kabod* at times.

I do the hand actions at church, but God cannot have my money, which represents my *kabod*. I am paid for my glory—which is this "highest flower" of my time and my efforts and my talents and skills and discipline.

Money is a token of my glory. And when I give my money to God, I am giving Him glory. He is the one who gave me the glory (power) to get wealth, and so my giving becomes this mystical act of self-consciousness wherein I come to terms with the reality of the Divine in my life— the most existential reality—that in Him I live, and move, and have my being.

Another application could be in our gifting—perhaps you are an articulate person, and if I asked you to write a letter to some poor downtrodden soul in your church, you could pen a letter of such moving encouragement that it would chase hell and all its demons out of this person's tormented life.

But in your prayers, or in times of devotion, or in worship, that God-given gift lies dormant. It's like you're shooting blanks—there's no *kabod*.

And it's as if God is saying, "Hey—give *Me* some of that glory that you have. I want your energy and focus."

God wants my hands and so I will lift them to Him, but He wants the rest of me too.

Worship has to do with the rest of us—often times the holdout places—in our hearts.

In my relationship with my wife, there cannot be any holdout places.

I can't say that I love her and simultaneously disallow access to the major treasures of my life.

An example of this is joint bank accounts: she has access to all of my money. All of it. It's terrifying. She's got my credit cards. She's on the bill of sale of our house. She has access.

You cannot say that you are in a relationship with God and then block Him out of all of the places that matter to you—that's not how intimate relationships work.

You can't say, "Jesus is my Lord and Lover and King, but mainly I'm His lord and lover and king, because we do all the things that I want to do and He's just gonna have to deal. He loves me anyways, because that's how 'grace' works."

No, biblical worship is worshipping God His way. We

are priests unto God—which means that we worship Him on His terms.

It's all about Him, not me. I'm a priest, bringing my sacrifices to Him to the designated place of His choosing, which is the church—His beloved bride, His body.

Worship on my terms is not acceptable worship and will be rejected.

Worship that is not God's way is ultimately worship of self, because I have projected onto Him and rejected His preferences.

And what I miss when I worship this way is God Himself.

The cost of not worshipping God *His* way is loss of His Presence.

And nothing is worth that.

Chapter Four

GOD HAS AN AMP TOO

In relationships, intimacy begets intimacy.

When you show up with the "avocado toast" as well as your attention, present-ness, and affection, it unlocks that other person's attention, present-ness, and affection. The avocado toast itself only gets you so far in a relationship—it's only a symbol that shows that you are paying attention and desiring to love that person the way they want to be loved.

And that symbol is significant—it's not insignificant—it matters, because once again it demonstrates that your head is in this thing. But present-ness, which is part of your glory, and access to the very best of you—the trajectory of your life, your dreams, bringing someone along in those things—that opens the other person up like a flower.

Glory begets glory.

When you give God *yad* with *kabod*, you get God with *kabod*.

When you worship God in His way, and there is a life behind those hands that are lifted—money, time, devotion, attention—the weightier things of your life—you get God *and* His glory.

Simply put, if you want God's glory, you need to give Him glory.

This is why David is turning his amp up to 11 in Psalm 57—because God has an amp and He can turn it up to 11 too.

There are so many Christians that are content with their fire insurance, and that's as far as they want to take things in God; they are saved, they feel like their life is sorted, and now they get to do whatever they want. They have a form of godliness but never experience the power of God.

We can have two people standing beside each other in worship, and both are lifting their hands to the Lord—giving Him the *yad*—but one lives a detached spirituality where God gets nothing else but this form, and the other imperfectly (because we rarely worship perfectly) gives the Lord glory—and there are radically different experiences in God.

Two people. Both raising hands. One gives glory with the hands. And that one experiences God's glory. The other does not. That's the story of the church.

Just because God is omnipresent does not mean that His glory or felt Presence is everywhere—why else would Jesus say, "Where two or three of you gather in My name, I'll be there."[24]

---

24. See Matthew 18:20.

God shows up uniquely in places where He is honored and desired.

James 4:8 reads, "Draw near to God, and he will draw near to you. Cleanse your hands, you sinners, and purify your hearts, you double-minded."

Now, God has already initiated this whole thing: He was the one calling out to Adam in the garden when Adam had hidden himself. Jesus is the Good Shepherd that seeks and saves that which is lost,[25] leaving the 99 to come after the 1.[26] God has already taken the first of many steps toward us.

But James is writing to the Christian community and saying, "Hey guys—in light of God's jealous desire to be with us—we need to draw near to Him. And as we do that, God will draw near to us."[27]

As I lean into the Lord, He leans into me.

As I bring my glory, He brings His glory.

This is the entire prize of worship for the church—the unique manifested glory of God. It's not a check in the mail, it's not a bank error in my favor, it's not a smoking hot spouse—it's the glory of His Presence that brings order to my chaos, an unimaginable wisdom and working that supersedes any imagination of a best-case scenario that I could dream up on my own.

The God of the Universe has a weight; He has an attention. And that is what I desire—not some prefabricated religious transaction, but rather an encounter with the glory of God that changes my face and my soul and

---

25. See Luke 19:10.
26. See Matthew 18:10–14.
27. See James 4:8.

my life. I want to be transformed—I need to be transformed—into the image of Jesus Christ. And we all have circumstances and situations that need the glory of God. It's holistic—*God, change me and everything around me—bring Your Kingdom rule to the divided and rebellious and fallen kingdoms of my heart and life.*

The author of the book of Hebrews is trying to give his worried Jewish audience a confidence that their prayers and sacrifices are reaching heaven. He wants them to have a boldness in coming before the throne of grace so that they can receive help in time of need. And the principle of sacrifice—particularly in the Old Testament context, to a people that would be intimately acquainted with the stories of the Bible—is meant to illicit an energetic response.

The principle of the acceptable sacrifice throughout the Old Testament is this: every acceptable sacrifice has a Divine Response.

Whenever an altar was built to God's specifications, and the sacrifice that was laid upon that altar was built to God's specifications, and the place of that altar and the sacrifice were to God's specifications, God would receive the sacrifice.

More importantly, where there was great "glory" poured upon the altar by the vassal (Israel or a leader)—for example, the dedication of Solomon's temple—the glory of the Lord would show up in a thickness and cloud. Often times, fire would fall upon an altar.[28]

And whenever an altar or sacrifice was not built to divine specifications, like Cain's offering that was just

---

28. See 2 Chronicles 7:1–22.

mailed in, God is faithful to reject the offering and not show up.

Every unacceptable sacrifice is rejected, and every acceptable sacrifice has a Divine Response!

For me, this gets me pumped about the gathering of the church, the giving of tithes, and the volunteering of my time for the Kingdom of God—because I know what He wants. I have His Word—an act of grace in and of itself.

I remember trying to figure out my wife when we were preliminarily sniffing each other out. I was interested but I didn't have a plan—I didn't know what she liked. I didn't know how to win her. I wanted to be winsome and capture her heart, but I had no revelation about her.

Many people in the ancient world were anxious about their spiritual life—they knew there was more to life than mere materiality, but they had no special revelation of God. An example of this spiritual anxiety is an Assyrian prayer called "Prayer to Every God" that was discovered in the ruins of Ashurbanipal's library in Ninevah, dating to 668–633 BC:

> May the fury of my lord's heart be quieted
> toward me.
> May the god who is not known be quieted
> toward me;
> May the goddess who is not known be
> quieted toward me.
> May the god whom I know or do not
> know be quieted toward me;

May the goddess whom I know or do not
know be quieted toward me.

My transgressions are many; great are my
sins.
The transgression which I have committed, indeed I do not know;
The sin which I have done, indeed I do
not know.
The forbidden thing which I have eaten,
indeed I do not know;
The prohibited place on which I have set
foot, indeed I do not know.
The lord in the anger of his heart looked
at me;
The god in the rage of his heart con-
fronted me;
When the goddess was angry with me, she
made me become ill.
The god whom I know or do not know has
oppressed me;
The goddess whom I know or do not know
has placed suffering upon me.

How long, O my goddess, whom I know
or do not know,
ere your hostile heart will be quieted?
Man is dumb; he knows nothing;
Mankind, everyone that exists,—what does
he know?

Whether he is committing sin or doing
good, he does not even know.
O my lord, do not cast your servant down;
He is plunged into the waters of a swamp;
take him by the hand.[29]

Christian's seem to take YHWH's revelation of Himself in Scripture—the most foundational part of our faith—for granted in their minds. And here we have these poor souls in the ancient Near East—burdened with anxiety over their complete spiritual darkness—begging for clarity on how to please the gods.

They don't even know what is right and wrong, but they are sure they are making a mess—I love the earnestness of the prayer.

Then YHWH goes to all this trouble of revealing Himself, and being detailed on how people should approach Him—the Old Testament is just a field guide on how to survive an encounter with God—God even writes some of His Law on stones with His own finger!

Next, consider the incarnation of Jesus Christ—birth, life as a human child, His ministry and ultimate death and resurrection. Think of the humility that God has shown in communicating and over-communicating (ad nauseum, you ever read Leviticus?) who He is and His ways—to the point of His own suffering and rejection.

God—in His great humility and grace—has revealed Himself.

---

29. Daniel Block, *For the Glory Of God: Recovering a Biblical Theology of Worship* (Grand Rapids: Baker Books, 2016), 34–35.

We know what pleases Him and displeases Him. We know what brings His glory and what quenches His Spirit.

What this all means is that I can have confidence in my worship as a New Testament priest. Through Jesus I can continually offer up sacrifices of praise to which He responds to, meaning that I can experience His glory continually.

And this makes church particularly magical, because the local church is where I am a "living stone, built up into a spiritual *house*, to be a holy priesthood, offering spiritual sacrifices acceptable to God through Jesus." It is the local church that Peter is addressing. It is the scattered local churches that the author of Hebrews is addressing, to whom he will write, ". . . not neglecting to meet together, as is the habit of some . . ." (10:25).

The church is supposed to be a place of glory because the priests are ministering glory to the Glorious One, who manifests His Presence by the Holy Spirit, who mediates the Presence of Jesus to the church.

As a priest I get excited out of my mind to gather with the church, because all of these little things (songs, lifting of hands, giving) that seem peripheral to the "consumer Christian" become central to the priestly Christian.

Understanding the priesthood and the sacrifices and the glory of God makes church like Disneyland for me. Let me explain what I mean:

My wife and I are obsessed with Disneyland. I remember when we first moved to California three years ago, we went to Disneyland and bought the top annual pass that a resident of California could hold. It had all access, no blackout dates, and tons of perks. We were beside our-selves giddy.

Disneyland is so different for us than other amuse-ment parks. Now, don't get me wrong—I love amusement parks—I'm a thrill-seeking, roller-coaster-riding nut job. I love drops and loops and bumps and sharp turns. But there's something more to Disneyland than just rides. And to be honest, Disneyland isn't exactly the most thrill-ing theme park with respect to hair-raising rides. But it's something way more important: it's magical.

You see, we know all the stories and characters and songs. We grew up with our imaginations running wild in the land of Pixar; the soundtrack of our early life was written by Alan Menken.

Every brick of Disneyland is sacred for us—there are no throwaways. We aren't just on a miniature train track in a poorly painted cart looking at cheesy cardboard min-iatures of a snowy city—no, we are soaring over snowy London with Peter, Wendy, James, and John. The ride is a magical medium—a kind of enchanted wardrobe—that has teleported us to another land.

I remember my mother telling me about how she cried when she first saw Buckingham Castle. She's read every biography on the Royal Family going back to the Tudors. She's obsessed, and the experience for her was immersive. Un-fazed tourists standing beside her snapped photos mat-ter-of-factly—Mum wept upon hallowed ground.

That's what church is supposed to be like.

Everything means something in the church—there are no throwaways.

And the challenge then is to resist how repetition can cause us to lose meaning.

But the gathering of the saints is to be anything but a bad middle school Christmas play that we endure. It's supposed to be a sacred connection with the Creator of the Universe.

The Protestant church needs to repent of consumerism and quickly adjust anything in its programming that promotes consumerism. Its congregants need to be taught about the great responsibility they have toward their churches—bringing glory so that the God of glory shows up.

Thankfully, God is not looking for perfection. If He was, He wouldn't bother being in relationship with us. But He is looking for a pulse—an imperfect lean.

When my wife has snapped her fingers in my face as I selfishly disengaged, tuning her out and dozing into deep thought—I awake and repent.

"Nathan—where are you?"

"I'm sorry, babe—please forgive me. I'm back—where were we?"

She looks at me, rolls her eyes, and lets out a sigh.

"I'm sorry—I lost you at the T-Rex attacking the velociraptors."

She begins to slowly crack a wry smile, "Okay—so then King Kong appears all of a sudden . . ."

Maybe you haven't been consistent in your giving, and today you say, "I'm sorry, Lord—I'm back."

Maybe you haven't been lifting your hands because you're "not a hand lifter," and you've been making worship all about you and not about what God delights in, and today you say, "I'm sorry, Lord—I'm back. I'm listening."

Maybe there are other places in your life—places of glory—where you know God is stirring you. The Holy Spirit has a giant yellow highlighter and He's marking places in your heart that He wants you to surrender, and today you say, "I'm sorry, Father—I'm back. I'm listening. I belong to You—this belongs to You."

And you're doing all of this because you don't want to live your life without God's Presence.

James says, "Cleanse your hands, you sinners" (4:8).

How do I cleanse my hands?

By giving them. What is given to the Lord is sanctified.

As in, "God, my hands have been building my plans and dreams and desires my whole life. They've been about my business. And today I surrender the work of my hands to You—I want to be about my Father's business. Cause me to delight to do Your will. Take my hands, Lord. They are Yours. I'm back, and I'm building Kingdom things."

James continues, "And purify your hearts, you double-minded."

As in, "God, I'm not doing this detached spiritual thing any longer, where I give You a part of me, but You never get the heart of me. By the grace of God and the power of the Holy Spirit at work in me, You will have access to every part of me. I give You my heart—the center of my being—with all of my worries and concerns. You will have my treasure, my glory, my time—the most important things to me. I surrender them all to You, because I need

Your glory, and my life as an act of worship is my reasonable act of worship anyways."

And lastly, if you need to repent of being a consumer and making church all about yourself, do that now, praying:

> *Father, forgive me. I repent for my selfishness and self-centeredness. Cleanse me of this unrighteous posture, and renew my vision of the church. Let me see her as You see her—Your precious bride, whom You desire to visit and build and make beautiful. Father, You are the prize. You have given me my priesthood as a gift, and I will make You my priority as I appear before You in the house of God. I will bring my sacrifices and minister to You, and I will minister to others, because this is what You have asked for. And I know that Your glory will fall upon the church as we worship You, and many will see and hear that the Lord is in this place. In Jesus's name, Amen.*

INTERLUDE

Chapter Five

THE ANOINTED CHURCH

Have you ever wondered what "anointing" is?

In Charismatic church culture, "the anointing" was the crème de la crème—the pièce de résistance—the collectively perceived highest value that church people assigned to something particularly spiritual.

"That song is so anointed."

"She is such an anointed singer."

"The anointing was flowing at that service."

I'd overhear adults make these kind of remarks any time they were impacted by something, and it was often referred to in moments where the music was exceptional.

And it always confused me because I couldn't tell what was anointing, but somehow they always knew— like there was an internal anointing detector they had received to which I was unaware. I was that Charismatic kid that always had annoying questions about everything, constantly asking for definitions—not because I was being facetious—but because I had genuine faith and wanted to know more about it.

Into my adult years the answers and definitions that I received about the anointing remained unsatisfactory. There didn't seem to be a cohesive idea behind what we called anointed. The best definitions I had heard were from a college lecture that Dr. Frank Damazio gave when I was a student in Portland, Oregon.[30]

As I began to study it, particularly as compared to gifting, I began to develop a fuller picture for what it meant—and I'm convinced that if Jesus of Nazareth was anointed by the Holy Spirit and "operated under" the anointing,[31] then our people and churches desperately need it too.

In this chapter, I want to discuss what the anointing is biblically, what its purposes are, and how both individuals and churches can walk in it.

ANOINTING IN THE OLD TESTAMENT

To anoint or be anointed in the Old Testament is simply "to pour oil or ointment onto a person in a ritualistic fashion."[32]

The anointing of David in 1 Samuel 16 immediately comes to mind for most of us, and is a super-clear example of anointing. David is a shepherd boy, the youngest son of his father Jesse, and is essentially an unformed teenage dirtbag—as far as anyone knows. The prophet Samuel is instructed by God to go down to the house of Jesse and anoint as future king the son of Jesse as the Lord instructs

---

30. Frank Damazio, "The Anointing Value," Passions and Values (class lecture, Portland Bible College, April 10, 2008).
31. See Acts 10:38.
32. Robert D. Culver, "Anoint, Anointed," in Walter A. Elwell (ed.), *Baker Encyclopedia of the Bible, Vol. 1* (Grand Rapids: Baker Book House, 1988), 116.

him (on the spot, Samuel doesn't know which son is to be king yet). Jesse calls all his sons, who stand before the prophet; they're a bunch of Chads and Todds—sporty, buff, handsome barstool studs.

"Surely one of these guys will do."

But God is radio silent, and Samuel can't figure it out. God's like, "I haven't chosen any of these guys."

Samuel asks Jesse an awkward question, "Is this all your sons?"

Jesse replies, "I mean, all but the black sheep of the family, my youngest named David who is a pansy song-writer and watches sheep all day while singing his emo songs to God" (NFV, Nathan Finochio Version).

That David is missing is odd; David even writes an odd lyric in Psalm 27:10 that insinuates some kind of estrange-ment. In ancient literature, hero stories are always accom-panied by grandiose prologues about the baby and his parents. We see this in Scripture often (Moses, Samson, John the Baptist, Jesus). For a character as central and developed as David, his parents are conspicuously miss-ing. Was he the child of an affair (Ps. 51:5)? Best we have is the book of Ruth, a story about David's great-grand-mother, probably included by the Davidic Dynasty Edi-tors to build a historic case for how special David's lineage is—that YHWH has been working behind the scenes to bring the house of David to Israel.

Upon hearing there is another son of Jesse, Samuel the prophet sends for him.

David shows up and God says, "This is the one."

Now David didn't look like much compared to his

brothers. And this is where God famously whispers to Samuel that He doesn't look on outward appearances, but rather on the heart.[33]

This story has been culturally formative for Charismatic Evangelicals when it comes to their perceptions and speech on the anointing: the general idea being that giftedness and forms only go so far, and that the anointing is the difference maker, and that God anoints people who have hearts for Him.

Anointing mythology (by mythology I mean "formative cultural story") generally centers around music in the Charismatic church because of the story of David. Music is mystical and powerful and seen as a medium by which the spiritual world breaks into the natural world in the Charismatic movement, once again because of passages like 2 Kings 3:15, where a prophet calls for a harpist, and as the harpist plays, "the hand of the LORD came upon him," or passages like 1 Samuel 16:14–23, where David plays his harp and Saul is relieved of the tormenting spirits.

Charismatics place a high value on "anointed musicians and music" to create spiritually heightened atmospheres that set the table for the manifestation of charisms. And I don't have a problem with any of these concepts necessarily. The Scriptures are clear that God is enthroned on the praises of His people (Ps. 22:3); that praise is where God sets up His special rule—another reason why the corporate gathering is so unique.

But as we look at other concepts of anointing in the

---

33. See 1 Samuel 16:7.

Old Testament, we begin to round out our theology on the anointing, and our concepts become more concrete as they are founded on directive prescriptions of behavior rather than narrative descriptions. And this matters, because building doctrine from narrative is dicey at best. For example, the hand of the Lord was on Samson whenever his hair was long. Should we call for a hairstylist to put in extensions, so that we may prophesy?

What we discover in Torah is that the priesthood involved people and things anointed for specific service. Robert Culver elaborates: "From ancient times the Hebrews inaugurated officers of their national community by pouring special oil on the head of the person designated for office. The same practice was used to set objects apart for special divine use."[34]

The oil that was used for the anointing of the priesthood and all of the furniture of the tabernacle was made of a special mixture that God chose Himself, and it was not to be replicated for anything else. In Exodus 30:32–33, YHWH stipulates, "It shall not be poured on the body of an ordinary person. . . . It is holy. . . . Whoever compounds any like it or whoever puts any of it on an outsider shall be cut off from his people."

The concept of "holy" had to do with sacred things that were "set apart." Holy people and holy things were anointed, and once they were anointed, they were "set apart" for specific sacred tasks—for the purposes of YHWH.

YHWH had a game plan and He needed people

---

34. Culver, "Anoint, Anointed," 116.

whose entire lives were committed to accomplishing His will in the earth. He needed "lifelong staffers" (that we call priests) who understood His Special Revelation in Torah, were able to articulate exactly what YHWH wanted done in the Israel nation, and involved themselves in the special purposes of YHWH for the nation (tabernacle care, prayers, sacrifices, worship, discipling of other priests).

An anointed person in the Old Testament was anointed for YHWH's purposes, not their own.

They were chosen by YHWH—set apart from other people within the covenant community—to carry out specific offices and functions.

David was not anointed to play the harp, although he was gifted by God and ultimately stewarded that gift—a gift that the Holy Spirit would use to write the canon of Scripture. David was anointed to be King of Israel (and within that, to be a certain kind of king).

Paul the apostle wasn't anointed to write books, but theological writing was obviously a gift that he developed throughout his life; Paul was anointed by Jesus to be an apostle to the church (and within that, to be a certain kind of apostle).

ANOINTING IN THE NEW TESTAMENT

The first example of anointing in the New Testament is the anointing of Jesus of Nazareth.

In Luke 3, we see Jesus at His baptism, and the Holy Spirit "descended on him" (v. 22); then in Luke 4, we see Jesus "full of the Holy Spirit" and "led by the Spirit" (v. 1) into the wilderness for the temptation.

Jesus does what Adam and Israel could not in forty days, and overcomes all these temptations by the help of the Holy Spirit.

After the wilderness temptation, we see Jesus emerge "in the power of the Spirit" (Luke 4:14); we are watching an increased level of Spirit enablement in such a short time, from baptism to victory over the devil. And the ministry of the Spirit to Jesus climaxes in this passage, where Jesus preaches His first sermon after entering the ministry. He's at His local synagogue in Nazareth where He grew up, and He stands up and reads Isaiah:

> "The Spirit of the Lord is on me, because
> he has anointed me to proclaim good news
> to the poor. He has sent me to proclaim
> freedom for the prisoners and recovery of
> sight for the blind, to set the oppressed free,
> to proclaim the year of the Lord's favor."
> (Luke 4:18–19 NIV)

Jesus is now anointed—He's stepped into His mission—His life has one direction now, to fulfill the purpose of His incarnation through the revelation of Himself as Messiah. He will reveal who He is through His preaching and miracles which verify who He is. He will target the oppressive work of the devil by His powerful deliverance and healing ministry; He will minister hope to the poor in spirit, those who think God is far away from them; He will open the eyes of the spiritual and physical blind, demonstrating that He is God (power over nature) and Messiah (the hope of Israel incarnate).

The anointing of the Holy Spirit in Jesus's life meant that His entire life and focus had changed from being Mary's son to God's Son, to family purposes (Mary at the wedding in Cana) to His Father's purposes. Before this moment, He will save face for His mother's side of the family at a wedding where the groom's family has run out of wine—a socially catastrophic moment. Jesus Himself even tells His mother, "Woman—what does this have to do with me? My hour has not yet come" (John 2:4). Commentators often mention how informal His language is toward His mother,[35] but this will be the last time He's asked to fill up the sugar jar with His Jesus powers (bear with my folly).

And this is the same calling with which Jesus's disciples will be called: everything, including their businesses and natural families, will become peripheral to this setting apart.

Jesus is called Christ (Greek, "anointed one") because He was the Messiah (Hebrew, "anointed one"). Christians are "anointed ones." John will write to the church and explain that the reason people left the church was because they were not anointed ones, and that the anointing helps the church understand and hold onto the truth (see 1 John 2:19–21). The anointed ones, in John's mind, are people who hold onto the truth about Jesus, the Anointed One.

Both Paul (2 Cor. 6:17) and Peter (1 Pet. 1:16) will

---

35. See Gerald L. Borchert, *John 1–11* (Nashville: Broadman & Holman Publishers, 1996), 154–55; D. A. Carson, *The Gospel According to John* (Grand Rapids: Eerdmans, 1991), 170.

tease out this more robust, biblical idea of anointing in their letters to the churches. Remembering that anointing separated the priesthood and vessels for use in the holy (separated) things in the tabernacle, and keeping in mind that Peter calls the church a priesthood, we can make the following general statement about the anointing as it pertains to Christians:

> **Christians are anointed by the Holy Spirit, separated from the business of the world for the work of the ministry, which is worship to God, building of the church, and reaching the world.**

Every Christian is separated to God for His purposes. Thus, every Christian is anointed.

Now, within that general separation or anointing, there are specific anointings. Not everyone is anointed by the Holy Spirit for what I like to call "ascension gift ministries" (see Eph. 4:11), or to build a business that finances the Kingdom, or raise godly offspring. Sometimes we call this calling, but it has more to do than calling in a secular sense.

This is where we need to begin to distinguish between gifting and anointing, for sake of clarity, and why I first found Dr. Frank Damazio's lecture on this years ago to be helpful; he also has an extensive teaching on the anointing in his book *The Making of a Leader*.[36]

---

36. Frank Damazio, *The Making of a Leader* (Portland, OR: City Bible, 1988), 283–300.

ANOINTING VS. GIFTING

Anointing and gifting are both from God.

Anointing and gifting both need to be stewarded.

The gift is given without repentance—you can be gifted by God and serve the devil with it, and God doesn't take that gift away; but the anointing is for a specific purpose: you can't serve the devil with your anointing.

Thus, the gift is corruptible, but the anointing is incorruptible, because the anointing only ever accomplishes the purposes of God.

The gift—because it is given freely to the human spirit—is an extension of the human spirit and soul; it is nurtured by the expanse of the human soul through all of the troubles and darkness and brightness and light of the soul. All of the seasons of the soul can serve to grow the gift, but the anointing is not a part of the human spirit or soul, it comes from the Holy Spirit and stays upon the human spirit so long as the purposes of God are being served. It is a separation to purpose.

Saul was anointed king of Israel, but when he began to serve his own purposes instead of God's, the kingdom was stolen from him and another was anointed. Saul remained anointed as long as he was king, because the anointing has to do with the separation to purpose, not the person (he couldn't just stop being king). But while he was serving in the office, another had been anointed for his office.

The anointing doesn't belong to you; it belongs to God and comes upon you as long as you are separated to

God for His purposes. In 1 Kings 2:27, Solomon banishes Abiathar from the priesthood—Abiathar was anointed (separated) to the priesthood, yet when he began to build another kingdom, that priesthood was removed from him—thus the anointing. He was no longer anointed.

The gift can serve and build up self—platforms, businesses—but the anointing always builds Christ; we can certainly glorify God with our gifts and build other people up with our gifts, but the anointing is always accomplishing the purposes of God, which are to form Christ.

The gift can be a vehicle for the anointing: if I am called to build the church, and my gift is how I build the church, I am operating in the anointing; but *the anointing is not a vehicle for my gift*—as if my gift is more important than the purposes of God.

Keeping that in mind, while the gift causes "manifestation" or "self-actualization," the anointing is often pulling us in the opposite direction, toward the cross where we die. The gift is the birth of self, the anointing causes the death of self.

The gift is chiefly directed and developed by human will, whereas the anointing is directed and developed by the Spirit of God.

Pastor Frank, in his lecture, says, "The gift gives goosebumps, the anointing breaks the yoke."

The gift inspires, but the anointing transforms.

D. L. Moody is a great example of this. It is said that he was a boring speaker, comparatively to the great orators of his time, like Spurgeon. But when he would speak, people would weep under the conviction of the Holy

Spirit, and the manifest Presence of the Spirit was felt in the room.[37]

Moody wasn't gifted, but he was anointed.

The Corinthian church is an incredible case study in all of this: they are the spiritually gifted church. But because they have no love (no understanding of the purpose of their existence and what their gifts should ultimately be accomplishing), their church is dead and dying.

My gifts are from God, and I can use them to build myself or for Kingdom purposes—for that which I was anointed by the Holy Spirit to accomplish.

But my ultimate concern needs to be the anointing, and I only grow aware of and cultivate the anointing of God on my life as I give myself to the things of God— things that awaken and feed my prophetic imagination. As I pray, read the Scripture, worship God, and gather with the saints, something inside of me begins to stir. My attention is captured; I've become aware of invisible things; I become cognizant of what God has called me to.

Now I'm cultivating the anointing: I'm beginning to understand the will of God because I'm being transformed by the renewal of my mind. I'm able to discern

---

37. Moody biographer Lyle W. Dorsett says of Mr. Moody, "Moody's power to communicate with souls at the deepest levels transcended all natural boundaries, including those of class and nationality." Lyle tells the story of how Woodrow Wilson, prior to his presidency, experienced Moody's power to communicate the gospel in a barbershop. He quotes Wilson's account of the event, who said, "sitting in the chair . . . I became aware that a personality entered the room. A man had come quietly in upon the same errand as myself and sat in the chair next to me. Every word he uttered . . . showed a personal and vital interest in the man who was serving him. . . . I was aware that I had attended an evangelist service, because Mr. Moody was in the next chair. I purposely lingered in the room after he left and noted the singular effects his visit had upon the barbers in the shop. They talked in undertones. They did not know his name, but they knew something had elevated their thought. And I felt that I left that place as I should have left a place of worship." See John McDowell et al., *What D. L. Moody Means to Me: An Anthology of Appreciations and Appraisals of the Beloved Founder of the Northfield Schools* (E. Northfield, MA: The Northfield Schools, 1931), 23 in Lyle W. Dorsett, *A Passion for Souls: The Life of D. L. Moody* (Chicago: Moody Publishers, 1997), 19.

what is good and acceptable and perfect because I'm growing in the anointing of the Spirit, a grounding in the truth.

The anointing is understood acutely as I am discipled, as the mind of Christ is formed in me.

Now I am certain of my reason for living. I can articulate with dictionary definition what it is that I am anointed for.

THE ANOINTED CHURCH

I believe that churches are anointed for "general service" and "specific service."

When a congregation begins to uncover what they are anointed for, that's when they begin to make incredible impact.

Jesus's first sermon in Nazareth made incredible impact: He almost got thrown off a cliff![38]

His anointed sermon—the announcement of His ministry—made waves throughout His community, to the point that He was rejected there.

Economic success or sociological favor aren't the ultimate measures of the anointing, as we learn from Jesus's first sermon. Maybe the anointing on your life and on your church is meant to shake the community you are in.

And this is how language like "prophetic assignment" is so helpful: it helps identify what you are anointed for.

To be sure, the anointing will always cause your life or church to cut through the white noise: it will make

---

38. See Luke 4:28–30.

waves—good or bad! But it will accomplish the will of God.

The anointing always accomplishes the will of God. Thus, tapping into what you believe to be your prophetic destiny or prophetic assignment—your *raison d'être*—is crucial.

NEW YORK CITY, THE GREAT TRANSFORMER

When I moved to New York City in 2010, I thought I was going to be a musician. I was musically gifted but I was anointed to build the church. That is what I have been anointed for.

I had avoided teaching and speaking because I never felt like I fit in; I couldn't stand the song and dance of the Charismatic pulpits in which I was raised. Additionally, I wasn't a philosophical match for the movement I was a part of. I never imagined in a million years that I would be running a theology school, traveling around the world teaching at churches, writing books, and doing ministry in this way. I thought perhaps I would do music ministry, but that was mainly because I loved music and I was good at it.

When I went to New York, my music career fell apart.

I was devastated.

Every door for music seemed to have more locks and chains and bolts than Jacob Marley.

I became very discouraged, cynical, and resentful— this led to deep depression.

I was newly married, living in another country, no job, and unsure what to do.

But I felt like I wasn't supposed to go anywhere. I was supposed to be stuck.

Several months after my music stuff soured, I was offered a job by some pastors who took pity on me. They needed someone to run a weekly Bible class for new converts, and I needed to pay my rent. I agreed.

I had never done this and thought it would be temporary. But I put my heart and soul into it.

I wrote fourteen Bible College courses over the next four years for the Monday night Evening College. After a year of doing this, the pastor asked me to start speaking on Sundays. I had spoken on a Sunday maybe five times in my life, and it always bombed. I was terrified.

The church was fairly large and they were used to having world-class speakers every Sunday. I was this neurotic Bible nerd who made nervous jokes and spoke in a stream-of-consciousness sort of manner.

I remember bawling my eyes out in the prep room after my first service. People came to see someone awesome and they got me, and I didn't even want to be doing this. So many others had this vision for their life. Not me. I didn't want to be a preacher. I didn't want to be broke like my dad.

My dad was an itinerant preacher in Canada for years and then pastored a church for almost twenty-five years in rural Ontario. We weren't poor but we were broke. The ministry meant we couldn't afford a trip to Disneyworld like every other kid in our church; it meant we drove old cars; it meant that we never got to go to a restaurant. It meant that we had to live in the church offices because the church couldn't afford to pay my dad properly.

So naturally I chose being a musician—surely *that's* the way to make money!

Here I am, stuck in NYC, teaching the Bible like my dad, resenting that I have to do this for nothing (I made 40K a year living in Manhattan with a wife who didn't work), surrounded by successful people. It was the success of my friends that hurt the most—made me feel like the idiot outsider all over again. I was happy for them but sad for me.

But the Lord is my Shepherd, and He leads me.

And I don't get to decide what I am anointed for, my Shepherd does.

As I began to teach, the Lord began to open doors to us and provision began to come into our lives. I began to get ideas about teaching; I began to build relationships with people.

I stopped thinking of myself as a musician. That was the hardest part, and sometimes still is, because I love music so much. I'm obsessed with it. But the Lord began to stir up my prophetic imagination for what He has anointed me for and called me to.

And as I have leaned into what I believe I am anointed for specifically, it has refined me and my ministry. Sometimes I've felt like Jesus and the five thousand; sometimes I've felt like Jesus at Nazareth and the angry crowd.

But what we see happening is the formation of Christ through our ministry; we believe that churches are supplied and strengthened, leaders are resourced and encouraged in their calling, and that we are operating in the anointing.

I don't always feel gifted for what I am doing, but I know that I am doing what God wants me to do.

I want to close this section by making three statements on the anointing as it pertains to the church:

1. **The prophetic identity of a church matters.** Every church in a locality serves a different purpose: Frank Damazio has written a fantastic book on this called *The Gate Church*.[39] But finding what you are anointed for is what will cause provision and people to come to you. As a church takes definition, that is where the right people show up and the wrong people leave. Every church will be pruned—you're pruned if you do, and pruned if you don't. Pruning should happen because of the anointing, not because of your gifting. If we make our churches or ministries about our gifting, we never really find the right people because the right people are attracted to purpose, and that's what the anointing is about.

2. **The prophetic identity of a church is cultivated.** Too many churches are opened because someone wants to grow a church or be a pastor or doesn't like how the church they attended "did church." Then we get these undefinable de facto churches where they say a lot but don't mean a

39. Frank Damazio, *The Gate Church* (Portland, OR: City Christian Publishing, 2003).

lot; they have the forms but take no form. Human beings are desperately looking to be a part of something that matters. And if we cannot define our prophetic vision—what we are anointed for—we will leave our people purposeless. They will sit in our churches untrained, bored, consumeristic, waiting to find a church that will disciple them. This is why we have to bring back church membership, Training Tracks, etc., anything with any kind of sustained intentionality. Catholics make new members take classes for a year before their first communion; the best many of us have is four weeks. Now, four weeks is better than nothing. But we need to think again in terms of catechism. If you will build your people and give them a vision, you will build something remarkable. Tell your people why they are set apart. And tell them how they can be about the business of being set apart.

3. **We need to get away from a focus on gifts and an emphasis on priesthood**. All of this self-help, Enneagram, Myers-Briggs, be-all-you-can-be, negotiate-the-terrifying-world-of-relationships stuff does not build the Kingdom, and I will argue that it doesn't build people. What builds people is purpose; and Kingdom purposes often have more to do with people ridding themselves of their own ambitions than not. Discipleship used to mean taking up the cross; now it means being a great listener and going for nature walks. There is no doubt that (to quote myself) spiritual

maturity does not happen outside the context of relationships; but spiritual maturity has to do with understanding God's redemptive plan in the earth, and why the church even exists. The priesthood is a paradigm shift because it brings a new identity, a new job, a new posture, and a new language. We don't serve at churches because we are gifted, we serve at churches because we are priests who have a heart for the Kingdom of God.

The anointed church, then, makes a radical shift from self-obsession to God obsession; it turns from pseudo-self-development to holy calling; it pivots from self-centered consumerism to an outward-focused priesthood; it transforms detached spiritualism into a realized eschatology and earthy ecclesiology.

It makes weak churches killer churches.

Chapter Six

THE IMMOVEABLE
CHURCH

I lived in New York City for eight years.

I was in Soho for two years, the East Village for three years, the West Village for one year, and Williamsburg for two years. I knew Manhattan pretty well and had friends all over the island.

One thing I never did was ride a bike.

I never did it in Central Park; never borrowed a friend's bike; never wanted to ride a bike, and had zero interest in being on two wheels for any amount of time in NYC.

First reason was that we had a key volunteer in our church die on a bicycle when she was hit by a garbage truck—that was enough for my disposition toward cycling in the city to be firmly cemented.

My brother once witnessed a biker get creamed by a cab driver. I've witnessed the aftermath several times. You've gotta be nuts to ride a bike on the Avenues.

Second reason was that bicycles were always getting stolen or thrashed in the streets. You ride that thing to work and an hour later some hipster is riding it across the Williamsburg Bridge back to Bushwick. Because what does a hipster's girlfriend get for her birthday? Your bike.

I remember watching some live comedy on TV years ago where a dude wanted to show just how little New Yorkers care about bikes being stolen. He chained his own bike up to a tree and had the camera crew video him breaking through the chain. He used bolt-cutters, a lock pick, and even got out a little buzz saw—sparks were flying everywhere as he's buzzing through this chain—and nobody cared.

Even a cop walked by while he was buzzing and just kept walking. It was hilarious.

The streets are littered with the ghosts of former bicycles: a piece of a frame with no wheels or pedals chained to a bike stand; a back wheel missing the rest of the bike bound alone to a pole.

New York City is hard on bikes.

I like how Paul the apostle summarizes our entire faith into three words in 1 Corinthians 13:13—*faith, hope,* and *love*. And it seems that he uses this tripartite axiom as a diagnostic when writing to the churches, because these three essentials of our faith are what bind us together.

If we were to liken Christian spirituality to a bicycle—a vehicle with basic components that all work together to create momentum—I would say that faith is the basic framework, hope is the pedals and chain mechanism, and love is the steering apparatus.

Faith is the basic framework in that it's the design of the thing—the genius in the layout. Faith is the construction and what holds everything together.

Hope is what gets you out of bed in the morning—it's what you look forward to. Hope is the term often used by theologians when describing eschatology, the culmination of all things. Christians have a hope that Christ will return and set the world right, and that they will live with Him in the New Creation, and that the New Creation will make these present troubles pale in comparison. Thus, hope is what gives the Christian energy and endurance: it powers the Christian, and gives him movement. Hope is the pedal and corresponding chain mechanism.

And last but certainly not least, love is the purpose or goal of the whole thing—moving toward love. Love is the direction of the bicycle itself, powered by hope, held together by faith, with the aim being love. Love is the steering mechanism that reminds us we are going somewhere with this whole thing, and that direction really matters.

Faith is the frame, hope is the chain, love is the aim.

As I said before, Paul will use this concept to diagnose the problems of each church he is responsible for.

The Romans need to understand faith.

The Thessalonians need to understand hope.

The Corinthians need to understand love.

Each of these churches face unique challenges, and they risk breaking apart and losing their unity and purpose as a church if they neglect one of these theological issues that are immensely practical, so much so that they are destroying the church.

THE ROMANS

At the time of Paul's writing, the church in Rome is an ethnically divided church that refuses to fellowship with one another. The Roman church has allowed external societal attitudes and Judaic postures peripheral to Christianity to define how they think about one another.

Anti-Semitism was rampant in Rome: Tiberius (AD 19) and Claudius (AD 49) had both expelled the Jews out of Rome before the writing of this letter.[40] We read about Claudius's expulsion of the Jews in Rome in Acts 18, the occasion for Priscilla and Aquila coming to Corinth.

The genesis of the Roman Christian church is fascinating: scholars speculate that Jews from Rome must have been present in Jerusalem for the Passover when the Holy Spirit was poured out on the church and three thousand were added that day.[41]

It was the lifelong duty of a male Jew of the Diaspora (a Jew living abroad) to pilgrimage to Jerusalem once in his life for Passover. These Jews lived all over the world and spoke foreign languages. When Peter and the others started to speak in tongues, proclaiming the gospel in foreign languages, these Jews of the Diaspora heard their native tongues declaring the story of Jesus and were saved. These men would have traveled back to their hometowns

---

40. For more on the life of Tiberius and Claudius, see David Potter, *The Emperors of Rome* (London, UK: Quercus, 2013). Kruse notes that Paul believed that Gentile believers in Rome had negative attitudes toward the Jews that began to occur during the edict of Claudius in AD 49, under which Jews were expelled to Rome. See Colin G. Kruse, *Romans.* Pillar New Testament Commentary Series (Grand Rapids: Eerdmans, 2012), 435.

41. Kruse notes, "The Christian community in Rome probably owed its foundation to the work of Christian travelers, immigrants, and merchants, some of whom may have been present in Jerusalem on the Day of Pentecost (cf. Acts 2:10) and were therefore either Jews or proselytes." See Kruse, *Romans,* 2.

and planted new Jesus communities that were primarily Jewish culturally, being that they were founded by Jews.

As Gentiles began to join their communities, the Jews wanted the Gentiles to observe kosher laws and circumcision. For a time this may have worked, but with the expulsion of the Jews from Rome, Gentile Romans now ran the church. And with all of the visiting ministries from around the Mediterranean carrying news that the Gentiles were free to eat and drink what they wanted by faith, and were not required to be circumcised, the Roman church began to implement these newfound liberties in Christ.

When the Jews returned to Rome after Claudius had ceased to rule in AD 54,[42] they found the Gentiles swinging from the chandeliers, violating their most sacred rules: kosher law and circumcision were everything to a Jew.

The Jews threw a huge fit.

But the Gentiles weren't helping any: Roman culture saw Jews as deeply problematic, refusing to bend or change, always stirring up trouble over their religious beliefs and identity. Rather than seeking to understand, the Gentiles rubbed their liberties in the Jews' faces.

Paul has to write to this divided church and help them understand one another, and the way he'll get there is by writing an elaborate doctrine on the nature of faith.

In Romans 1, Paul will explain that Gentiles are in trouble and need Jesus.

In Romans 2, Paul will explain that Jews are in trouble and need Jesus.

---

42. See Robert Jewett, *Romans: A Commentary on the Book of Romans* (Minneapolis: Augsburg Fortress, 2007), 353.

Romans 3 summarizes, "All have sinned and fall short of the glory of God" (3:23).

Then in Romans 4:10, Paul will begin to talk about Abraham, and he'll pose a question to the Jews: Was Abraham justified by faith *before* or *after* he was circumcised? The Jews will beat him to the punchline: he was justified by faith before he was circumcised.

Paul is able to establish an Old Testament precedent for righteousness apart from the Law: this is a huge deal for the Jews, because Abraham is a towering father of faith—and if Abraham was called "righteous" while he was yet uncircumcised, that's significant.

Paul will continue to develop this thought by explaining that works of the Law don't justify us, but rather faith in God does. Paul is explaining to the Jews that kosher law and circumcision are not matters of salvation, because they weren't for Abraham and they aren't prerequisites for the justification that comes from faith in Jesus Christ. That's a double-pronged argument that will win the Jewish Christians over quick.

But what about their sense of duty before God?

Some of them have emotional attachments to kosher law: they still feel like they are breaking God's law if they eat Roman meat (not killed properly and probably offered to idols) or drink Roman wine (the production of which used non-kosher animal products as well as blood). Their conscience condemns them.[43]

---

43. Leon Morris argues that there were a likely a number of Torah-keeping Gentiles having the same issue. He notes, "On the other hand, some Gentile Christians, finding in their Bible (Greek Old Testament) food-restrictions imposed by divine authority, argued that these restrictions retained their force and should be complied with." See F. F. Bruce, *Romans: An Introduction and Commentary* (Downers Grove, IL: IVP Academic, 1985), 250.

Paul will outline the practicalities of faith in Romans 14. We are justified by faith, and we are called to live lives of faith. We never stop hearing God—like Abraham—but continually need to rely on His revelation to us, the source of all faith, because faith comes by hearing (Rom. 10:17).

What can heal a church that is divided because they refuse to eat the same food together, because these cultural issues are actually faith issues?

Understanding the nature of faith.

If I have faith to drink wine, it is okay for me to drink wine; but if my Christian brother does not have faith to drink wine, and his conscience condemns him, I must not try to press my strong faith onto him—because whatever is not of faith is sin. And I don't want to cause my brother to sin.

What God has said to me may not be what God has said to him—faith comes by hearing.

I may be called to liberties that he is not called to; God is the one who knows how to cause my Christian brother to stand. And God will cause him to stand. And my Christian brother might be called to liberties that I am not called to: that's between him and God.

I am not his master, and he must give account to God—he is another man's servant. Thus, I cannot judge him. And he can't judge me, either. We both give account to God.

So if I have faith for drinking Roman wine, I must keep that between myself and God—and practice that liberty and strong faith that I have out of my weaker brother's eyesight. I should not invite him over for dinner and then break out the Chianti.

And when I come over to his house, he should not start up a conversation about how he thinks I need to sip my Yoo-Hoo in order to be closer to God, or condemn me behind my back because I watch *Harry Potter*.

The TV shows that I watch are none of your business; they are between myself and God. And the music that you listen to is none of my business; it's between you and God. Because I understand how faith works, I don't judge you and you don't judge me.

We weren't saved by works, and our faith isn't perfected in the flesh.

And in this way, we can set aside our issues of faith because we understand that we weren't justified by works—these issues that are separating us aren't as important as we thought they were.

The Romans are to reject anti-Semitism and see the value and rich history that the Jews bring to the table with respect to the oracles of God (Romans 9–11), and the Jews are to reject national pride that leads to arrogance on peripheral issues that ultimately mean nothing. The Romans don't have to be Jewish and the Jews don't have to be Roman, because it doesn't save you.

But the church must be united in faith, and so if that means eating beans and bread when we visit the Jews or they visit us—who are weaker in faith—then that's what we will do. And we will also pray that they get a stronger revelation—like Paul—that these things mean nothing, and that they can let go of these cultural signposts as their ultimate definers, and begin to allow the gospel to permeate every part of their being.

Because the gospel is about the weak being made strong.

Paul will reverse the weak/strong hierarchy on the Jews—who think they are strong because they are the ones who have the history and Scriptures on their side—when, really, they have become the weak ones who complain about everything and need to learn Christ.

Strong faith—understanding the framework of salvation—unites the divided Roman church while challenging its weaker members to grow in a uniting faith.

Cultural concessions are not given much lasting power; they are called weak.

Immoveable churches rely on the clear message of faith to unite and build, not peripherals that ultimately lead nowhere. Peripheral cultural concessions are not legislated into the Roman church in order to bring about a temporary peace: a mandate to stop judging other people's faith issues is legislated.

Notice how Paul conducts diversity training in Romans 9–11 for the Gentiles, who have allowed the syncretistic Roman vision to rob the Jews of their dignity as the people of God. Nowhere else in Scripture will Paul do this, however: this is strictly a Jewish thing because they are a special people and the Gentiles simply are not.

The diversity training that we see in Romans 9–11 is about Israel's history with God—not as the oppressed subjugates of an imperialistic world order—but as the custodians of the divine history, the Law and Prophets.

What is special about the Jews is their proximity to YHWH, not their position in the social order.

Paul is saying, "Hey you, Gentiles, I know that Jew-hating is popular at the moment, but you're gonna wanna get to know these guys—they'll help you navigate the Scriptures. They understand the holy things, and you need to respect their vast knowledge and experience. So turn your dishonor into honor, because of the gift that these people are—especially when they come to faith. They are the root of this tree that you've been grafted into!"

Paul does not argue that the Romans should build inroads with the Jews based on Marxian "intersectionality";[44] he doesn't demand that a Zacchaeus fund be created to restore the finances the Jews would've lost at the hands of the imperial magistrates during the recent expulsion; he doesn't insist that "without restoration there can be no reconciliation"; he doesn't demand that Roman leaders de-platform themselves in favor of a Jewish leadership; he doesn't implement a Diversity, Equity, and Inclusion program that creates artificial peace; he doesn't lecture about how representation matters for the Jews and create quotas for leadership; he doesn't theologize that "God is with the down-and-outers" and that the Jews are the most marginalized group in the city and empire; all of these talking points are shifting sands and don't make for strong foundations.

Paul calls individuals to start believing properly and stop judging others immediately.

The fact that Paul writes a chapter each committed

---

44. Kimberlé Crenshaw, a law professor at Columbia and UCLA, coined the phrase *intersectionality*. She says, "Intersectionality is simply about how certain aspects of who you are will increase your access to the good things or your exposure to the bad things in life." See Katy Steinmetz, "She Coined the Term 'Intersectionality' Over 30 Years Ago. Here's What It Means to Her Today," *TIME*, February 20, 2020, https://time.com/5786710/kimberle-crenshaw-intersectionality/.

to articulating and condemning the unique sins of each culture group shows that Paul holds no punches.

Faith in the Charismatic world has come to be synonymous with simony and manifestation, but this is not what faith is. Faith is a coming home to one's mind and reason.

The Gentiles lost their minds when they rejected God as Creator, and become reprobate; the Jews lost their minds when they began to live reprobate lives, thinking that their ethnic contract with God could save them.

Paul will call them both back to their minds by laying again the foundations of faith.

An immoveable church is a church that refuses to build upon the foundations of the world, a church that rejects the trendy frameworks of what makes one virtuous and just, and rather establishes an equal footing of personal responsibility before God and each other.

The immoveable church is a church that is able to point out problems rationally, is able to establish doctrine reasonably, and is able to define "reasonable acts of worship."

The immoveable church is anchored by Scripture, not the latest philosophy.

The immoveable church is immoveable because it is obedient to faith—to the gospel—and the just live by faith.

THE CORINTHIANS

Corinth was destroyed by the Romans, and it was rumored that a few Greeks lived among the ruins, but Julius Caesar saw the potential of a strategic shipping center as well as a way to rid Rome of retired generals whose idle hands may lead to a coup. In one fell swoop, Caesar rid himself of would-be political rivals as well as built the most prosperous port city to date by re-establishing Corinth.[45]

The Roman generals took their soldiers and a massive population of freed slaves, turning the soldiers and slaves loose to industrialize and help build the town. Corinth was built by people who had never known personal liberty, and these soldiers and slaves became very rich very quick. All kinds of debauchery ensued.

Corinth was located on a two-mile isthmus—a track of land where the peninsula narrowed. Ships would arrive on its southern beachhead and portage their goods across the two-mile isthmus to abating ships on the northern harbor. In doing so, they would save a week of travel as well as the risk of traversing a treacherous horn where many shipwrecks occurred. Naturally, every single ship coming up from the south began to unload cargo in Corinth once the town was reconstructed. In no more than a hundred years, the town swelled to 700,000 residents.

And atop the Acropolis (a hill overlooking the city) stood the temple of Aphrodite, rumored to have had over a thousand prostitutes. Sailors would dock in the harbor, drink in the city, and then walk up to the Acropolis to indulge the flesh.

To "Corinthian" became a vulgar sexual expression in the Mediterranean—the city was world renowned for

---

45. See Roy E. Ciampa and Brian S. Rosner, *The First Letter to the Corinthians* (Grand Rapids: Eerdmans, 2010), 2.

its vice.[46]

Paul will have to rebuke the Corinthian church for allowing a man to sleep with his step-mom (1 Cor. 5:1), a sin unusual even for Corinth.

Beyond that, everyone is out for their own: there are factions, divisions, infightings, and selfish behaviors. The Corinthians don't see the church as something that they serve, but rather something that serves them.

They are the most spiritually gifted church (1 Cor. 1:7) and can prophesy the paint off the walls, but they see the gifts like the Enneagram—for self-service, to blab on and on and self-discover (14:30–31); they see the Table of the Lord as an opportunity to get hammered drunk (11:21); they are disorderly because of how self-focused they are (14:30) and it is hurting everyone at the church (11:17).

In short, the culture is leaking into the church—same problem in Rome and a common challenge in every church.

Paul will issue two of the sternest warnings in the New Testament in his first letter to the Corinthians, one in 3:16–17 and one in 11:29–30.

In chapter 3, Paul will address divisions in the church and say, "The church is God's temple: whoever destroys God's temple, God will destroy them" (vv. 16–17, paraphrased).

This passage has been proof-texted in the past as an

---

46. The one and only John MacArthur points this out. He notes, "Even to the pagan world the city was known for its moral corruption, so much so that in classic Greek *corinthiazesthai* ('to behave like a Corinthian') came to represent gross immorality and drunken debauchery. The name of the city became synonymous with moral depravity." See John MacArthur, *1 Corinthians*, The MacArthur New Testament Commentary (Chicago: Moody, 1984), vii. See also D. H. Madvig, "Corinth," *International Standard Bible Encyclopedia*, vol. 1 (Grand Rapids: Eerdmans, 1994), 773.

individualized reading, meaning that if someone commits suicide, God will destroy them. But we can easily conclude that this is not the case, seeing as Paul is addressing them corporately in the passage. Paul is taking aim at people who create trouble that divides the church, and is suggesting that God will destroy church dividers.

We have to understand the church as Jesus's bride, and thus His body. You can talk trash about me all you want, but if you start to talk trash about my wife, we are gonna have problems. In the same way, people who destroy the church do so at their own peril: Jesus won't allow the beloved that He died for to be destroyed.

These super-gifted people don't care about each other; they care about themselves.

The real miracle of this letter is that Paul wrote it at all.

If I were Paul and someone asked me about Corinth, I would claim that I'd never been there in my life. I would've dropped them like third period French.

Not Paul. He won't quit on them.

Another fascinating aspect of Paul's pastoral approach is that he doesn't shut down the gifts of the Spirit in their services. This is what most pastors would do. If the youth group starts acting crazy, "Shut 'er down!"

If the women's ministry goes off the walls? "Shut 'er down!"

Worship ministry starts thinking they're God's gift to the church? "Shut 'er down."

Some small groups go rogue and start having drinking parties? "Shut 'em down!"

And if the prophecy mic is literally being fought over

and people are prophesying over top of one another and everything turns into a Charismaniac mess? "Shut 'er down!"

Not Paul. Instead, he writes two of the clearest teachings on spiritual gifts and basically encourages them even more in their desire to manifest Spirit gifts in the local church (1 Corinthians 12 and 14). But then he sneaks 1 Corinthians 13—the love chapter—in between 1 Corinthians 12 (gifts) and 14 (gifts).

The gifts are the bread—love is the meat.

It's a love sandwich—because love is the direction of this whole thing.

Let's start reading in 1 Corinthians 14, coming out of the love chapter:

> Pursue love, and earnestly desire the spiritual gifts—especially that you may prophesy. For one who speaks in a tongue speaks not to men but to God; for no one understands him, but he utters mysteries in the Spirit. (vv. 1–2)

Firstly, Paul sets prophecy above every other gift—and he tells everyone in the church that they should all desire how to prophecy. Now, prophecy in the New Testament local church is a little different than our ideas or experiences sometimes. We often think of prophecy and conjure up some weird lady telling us who we'll marry or some sweaty guy in a suit telling us that we're gonna be a missionary to Uganda.

And while all of that may in fact happen and be true, that's not how Paul is about to define prophecy here in 1 Corinthians 14. But it's important to note that he has created a hierarchy, and he's saying that we need to earnestly desire spiritual gifts, especially prophecy.

Would you say that you earnestly desire to prophesy?

Because that is what the Holy Spirit is saying to you, right now.

Let's keep moving.

In the next bit, Paul says that the dude speaking in tongues is not understood—while he's yabba-dabba-doing, we're all excited for him and confused. He's speaking mysteries to God and nothing intelligible to us.

Paul continues in verse 3, "On the other hand, the one who prophesies speaks to people for their upbuilding and encouragement and consolation."

Here Paul defines local church prophecy: upbuilding, encouragement, and consolation. Or as my dad says, "Build up, stir up, cheer up."

Any Christian can do that and should do that—we can all find someone to build up in their faith, stir up in their calling and purposes in Jesus, and give them a smile. You can do this with your eyes wide open—and should. It requires you to look outside of yourself though and actually love others—notice them, care about them, stop thinking about yourself, and pay attention to their life.

Paul goes on in verses 4–5, "The one who speaks in a tongue builds up himself, but the one who prophesies builds up the church. Now I want you all to speak in tongues, but even more to prophesy."

CHRIST, WHO IS THE WISDOM OF GOD

Are you seeing this? Paul wants the way that they think about their spiritual gifts to totally change, and he creates a hierarchy of gifts in the church around what that gift accomplishes for others. Prophesy is greater and better because it builds the church up.

The Corinthians lack love, not spiritual gifting; but they don't understand that the whole point of their spiritual gifting is ultimately to build the church through love. The way for their church to be united and built up instead of fractured and destroyed is love expressed through interpersonal prophecy.

Thomas Aquinas called the Holy Spirit the Love of God,[47] and Jesus the Wisdom of God.[48]

The love of God is "poured into our hearts through the Holy Spirit," according to Romans 5:5.

It is the Holy Spirit, not Jesus, that lives in your heart; we are filled and indwelled by the Holy Spirit. Jesus is incarnated and is seated at the right hand of the Father, where He lives to make intercession for us. You and I are living in the Church Age—the Age of the Holy Spirit. Christ has ascended and the Spirit has come.

Think of how intimate that language of indwelling is for a moment—the Holy Spirit is inside of us. He's that much a part of us. When I do stupid stuff and He's whispering, "This is stupid, you goof," and I'm like, "I know it's so stupid," He doesn't leave. I grieve Him, but He

---

47. See Question XXXVII in Thomas Aquinas, *Summa Theologica*, trans. Fathers of the English Dominican Province (London: Burns Oates & Washbourne, n.d.).
48. See Question VII, Sixth Article in Aquinas, *Summa Theologica*. Note: Aquinas suggests this in a number of places throughout his *Summa Theologica*.

doesn't leave me. He is committed to me. He won't quit me. That's how much He loves me.

And this love of God—the Holy Spirit—wants to express His love for others. I have the love of God in me and that's why I love others—and this love wants to seep out of me and toward others.

Prophesy is the love of God pouring out of my mouth and toward—a method the Spirit uses to bind together and build the church.

I've learned to pay attention to these impressions of love I get for others. When I love someone, I should say something; when I am feeling love for someone, that is the Spirit prompting me to prophesy! To build up, stir up, and cheer up.

God's plan to build the church is you—it's the Spirit inside of you manifesting Himself in gifts that are others-directed.

You are our building program, a program of love.

In John 21, when Jesus restores Peter after he denies Jesus three times, Jesus asks Peter three times, "Do you love Me?"

The first time Peter responds, "You know that I love You."

Jesus says, "Feed My lambs." Or, build people in love, not lies—because "love rejoices with the truth"—but "speaking the truth in love that we may grow up into Him who is the head."[49]

Jesus asks Peter again, "Do you love Me?"

"Lord, this is getting embarrassing—I told you I love You."

---

49. See 1 Corinthians 13:6 and Ephesians 4:15.

"Feed My sheep."

A last time Jesus asks, "Peter—do you love Me?"

Peter is hurt this time: "Lord, You know all things; You know that I love You."

Jesus responds one last time, "Feed My sheep."

Jesus is saying, "If you love Me, build the church. Make loving the people of God your business. Your restoration is tied to your purpose. If you're grateful for My forgiveness and love, demonstrate it toward the church which is My sheep, My body, My bride."

I can't say that I love Jesus and hate the church.

I can't say that I love Jesus and not build up the church.

I can't say that I love Jesus and have no expressed love for the church.

If you love Jesus, show Him by your love (giving, serving, prophecy) toward the church.

Lovers build.

The immoveable church is a church whose love is predicated upon the framework of faith—not a wishy-washy worldly kind of love that multiplies kisses—but a love that rejoiced with the truth, is grounded in the truth of God's Word, whose framework is a framework of faith—a faith that has heard God and makes divine revelation the standard of all Christian love.

THE THESSALONIANS

Thessalonica received its prestigious free-city status when it sided in 31 BC with the victor of a Roman civil war: Octavian. Free cities were tax exempt—a massive relief in the Roman world. But they could lose this elite status if they refused to Romanize—to embrace the imperial decrees and doctrines of the Empire.[50]

Christianity, for the early years of its spread through the Roman world, had been thought of as a sect of Judaism. And while the Jews were a perpetual thorn in the side of the Empire (because of their refusal to assimilate and embrace Roman syncretism on a religious and cultural level), Judaism was still an official religion of the Empire. Free cities and colonies were required to ban unofficial religious meetings to outside the city walls.

The Jews began to figure out a way to suppress and destroy Christianity within the Roman Empire—by outing Christianity as a cult that is unconnected to Judaism. This would mean that Christianity could be legally rejected in the cities and colonies.

And this is the situation in Thessalonica: the Christians here are some of the most persecuted in the New Testament.[51]

The Jews in Thessalonica have told the city magistrates that if they allow Christianity to operate freely in the town, they might lose their free-city status. They have also told the city leaders that Christianity is one of those problematic "mystery cults" that stir up so much trouble in the Roman world. This has put the Thessalonian church in the crosshairs of just about everyone in the town.

---

50. See Gene L. Greene, *The Letters to the Thessalonians* (Grand Rapids: Eerdmans, 2002), 18–19. Greene notes, "Because of its support of Anthony and then Octavian, Thessalonica was recognized as a free city (*Thessalonice liberae condicionis*). Free-city status normally brough with it exemption from taxation, which was itself an honor of the highest category . . ."
51. Leon Morris notes that, as 1 Thessalonians moves into 2 Thessalonians, the problem of persecution "deepens." In other words, it only gets more intense. See Leon Morris, *1 and 2 Thessalonians* (Downers Grove, IL: IVP Press, 1984), 37.

The Thessalonian Christians are struggling. They are trying to find ways to avoid this political oppression. Many of them have given up on life and even stopped working. In their deep discouragement and anxiety, eschatology (the study of the end times) has become a forefront doctrine for them. But problematically, their eschatology is fueled by superstitions and fears.

Paul has to write several letters to them that outlines the return of Christ: he has to set them straight on some things.

In Christian theology, "hope" has to do with what is to come—with the return of Christ, resurrection from the dead, and eternal states.

But your eschatology affects your ecclesiology: what you believe about the end times directly affects what you believe about the church.

If you think the church is peripheral to God's ultimate plans for Israel, that will affect your preaching; if you think the church is going to grow smaller and weaker because of persecution and tribulation—to the point that the church is just white-knuckling its purposes in the last days until Jesus raptures it out as a relief—that will determine how you practically build and apply Scripture.

The Thessalonians think Jesus is coming back at any moment because their world is ending. They've become obsessed with eschatology to the point that they have become weird.

I don't know about you, but this COVID pandemic and now war in Europe has caused a lot of Christians to take to social media and be weird. People have stopped building church. They've stopped planting seed. They think the vaccine is the "mark of the beast." They think everything is the mark of the beast. They've become conspiracy theorists.

They read the book of Revelation using the "Newspaper Headline Interpretive Method": whatever bad thing is happening in the world, it must be in Revelation. Russia is the "bear from the north," and so on.

Aside from the fact that this is a highly arbitrary and subjective way to read Scripture, the church throughout history has rejected this way of reading Scripture. We tend to think we are important because we have the internet.

I like to ask folks that read Revelation this way whether or not they think the Second World War generation thought they were living in the end of days. Because that generation had lived through a previous world war, the Spanish Flu, a Great Depression, and now another giant war.

It turns out that Hitler wasn't the anti-Christ.

Simply put, anxiety is fear of future pain.

When we are scared of the future and what it might bring, we tend to get knots in our stomachs and crazy in our heads. We start to panic. Anxiety disorders begin to manifest.

Someone once said, "He who worries suffers twice."

The Thessalonians are crippled by anxiety and have become obsessed with self-created myth to the point that they are totally useless in the moment. Their Christian hope has been hijacked by fear and strange behavior.

Paul writes the most stunningly brilliant pastoral

directive: ". . . aspire to live quietly, and to mind your own affairs, and to work with your hands, as we instructed you" (1 Thess. 4:11).

Paul will address their questions about the return of Christ—some of the clearest teaching we have on the return of Christ is in this chapter. But what these people need is grounding.

Legend has it that someone asked Martin Luther once what he would do if he knew Jesus was coming back tomorrow. He replied, "Plant a tree."[52]

Paul tells the Thessalonians, "Live a normal life. Mind your own beeswax. Get a job—work with your own hands, like I told you before."

As in—live in the moment. Stop being useless to the church and city that you are called to. Get your hope back, stop being weird.

I'll never forget my first session with Dr. Arianna Brandolini in New York City. I was suffering from an anxiety disorder called panic disorder. My brain was on a feedback loop—I was stuck catastrophizing, continually imaging the worst possible outcome—and it was giving me knots in my stomach and fear in my mind like you wouldn't believe. It was hell.

Dr. Arianna was a volunteer at our church and she had been recommended to me as a psychologist. That day I came into her Manhattan office I was a hot mess. My body had become a teleportation device for my anxious

---

52. Whether Luther said this or not is kind of beside the point. I like the quote and I am sticking with it. For the dispute on whether he said it or not, see Martin Schloemann, *Luthers Apfelbäumchen: Ein Kapitel deutscher Mentalitätsgeschichte seit dem Zweiten Weltkrieg* (Göttingen: Vandenhoeck & Ruprecht, 1994), 246–51.

mind. I was all in my head.

I remember her opening up our session by telling me I was gonna be okay. I didn't believe her.

She told me that the basic idea of our therapy sessions was to break the rumination loop in my head by getting into my body. She said that you can't fight problems in your head with your head, but you gotta use your body.

My first homework that week was to scrunch my toes and notice my feet touching the pavement when I walked. I thought it was ridiculously expensive advice, but I was so desperate that I implemented the practice every day all day until our next session.

The next week she had me start to practice other "mindfulness techniques" and grounding techniques, like feeling myself against the back of my chair, the weight of my body in my seat. Once again, so silly and strange, but I did it.

As I began to pay attention to the moment that I was in, the feedback loop became interrupted and interrupted until it disappeared. This would be the beginning of a development freedom in many areas of my life.

And it all began with scrunching my toes.

Christian hope ultimately has to do with Jesus: Jesus is my future; He is my Living Hope. My Hope is a Person.

And that knowledge sustained me in my panic disorder—even though I was stuck in an anxiety loop, I didn't give up my basic hope in Jesus that caused me to push through the pain and believe God for better days.

But my anxiety loop became an attention hog: everything was about the fear and panic. It stole from my present and became quite the tyrant, dictating what I could and could not do every day.

You can have ultimate hope in Jesus but become a captive to panic and erratic behavior.

Paul's challenge to the politically charged, eschatologically confused church that has stopped sowing and building and working is the same paradoxical therapy that Dr. Arianna gave me: pay attention to your hands.

The immoveable church is a church that builds its way out of the pandemic.

The immoveable church sows its way to peace.

The immoveable church plants a tree in the midst of uncertainty, because it has been created for this moment.

Any disunity on these important but ultimately peripheral topics are cast aside as the church collectively decides to "lead a quiet life, mind its own business, and work with its hands . . ."

This doesn't mean we don't address issues, or investigate, or grow in our theology. Paul writes to clarify the Thessalonian eschatology.

But our hope comes from our planting.

Now abide faith, hope, and love—these will keep the church bound together, energized, built up, and headed in the right direction—steadfast, immoveable, always abounding in the work of the Lord.

SIDE B

Chapter Seven

THE SONG THAT NEVER ENDS

Every generation has its unique problems with Scripture. My grandparents' generation didn't have a problem with the idea that there was evil in the world, or that evil should be punished. Having lived through the Second World War, my grandma loved a good chat about sin and hell.

Her generation never bristled against Jesus's overt teaching on "eternal conscious punishment": that was the most easily digestible concept for them. After having lost her brother to the war, she was ironclad in her experience that evil existed and needed punishing, and that hell was necessary if God was just.

The idea that God could forgive—or that God was love—was a difficult doctrine to swallow.

How could God forgive Germany or Japan?

What about all the local boys who never came home to the neighborhood, their bodies littered across Europe and the Pacific?

What about all the Jews that had been slaughtered?

Grandma was a good Irish Catholic: she had faith in God, but aspects of Christian doctrine seemed difficult for her generation to fully buy into.

My generation—a generation that has never lived through the pain, anxiety, and bitterness of war—has the exact opposite problem: we could never believe that hell exists and that sin deserves to be punished.

We think people are victims, not sinners.

We see hell as the height of injustice, so we have these workarounds where we force some of the most clear and obvious texts on hell—where eternal conscious punishment is literally spelled out—to mean something entirely different. Our favorite Bible teachers are cultural masters that tend to sanitize Scripture rather than exegete it faithfully: they are on PR crusades to try and make the church more palatable.

Their experiences and instincts—their gut feelings that have been formed by the cultural milieu—ultimately become the guide, not Scripture.

The periphery of church history—not the bulk and center of it—becomes their foundation.

The periphery of Scripture—not the bulk and center of it—becomes their focus.

The mental gymnastics are laudable.

Point simply being that every generation has its formative experiences and myths, ours being no exception. Yes, we can never become totally unbiased or neutral, but that doesn't mean we cannot have increased objectivity, otherwise the truth is always out of reach, and nobody lives their life as if communication and interpretation is impossible. I'm sure even Jacques Derrida[53] ordered Chinese over the phone and expected his delivery to arrive to exact specifications. The goal is to become increasingly more unbiased or neutral as we become conscious of our biases and make an integrous commitment to the truth.

One of the ways I become aware of my generational and cultural biases as I read the writings of notable Christian thinkers from other generations—thinkers that walked in the paths of what we call Historic Christian Orthodoxy, a basic theological framework established at the church councils.

C. S. Lewis argued similarly for the reading of the literature of past generations. He writes,

> None of us can fully escape this blindness, but we shall certainly increase it, and weaken our guard against it, if we read only modern books. Where they are true they will give us truths which we half knew already. Where they are false they will aggravate the error with which we are already dangerously ill. The only palliative is to keep the clean sea breeze of the centuries blowing through our minds, and this can be done only by reading old books.[54]

---

53. Jacques Derrida is a French philosopher and considered the father of Deconstruction.
54. C. S. Lewis, "On the Reading of Old Books," in Sister Penelope Lawson's translation of *The Incarnation of the Word of God* (London, England: Geoffrey Bles, 1944). Reprinted in C. S. Lewis, *God in the Dock: Essays on Theology and Ethics*, ed. Walter Hooper (Grand Rapids: Eerdmans, 1970), 217–25.

G. K. Chesterton—Lewis's literary hero—outlines this idea of giving credence to tradition as an act of becoming self-conscious:

> Tradition means giving a vote to most obscure of all classes, our ancestors. It is the democracy of the dead. Tradition refuses to submit to the small and arrogant oligarchy of those who merely happen to be walking about. All democrats object to men being disqualified by the accident of birth; tradition objects to their being disqualified by the accident of death. Democracy tells us not to neglect a good man's opinion, even if he is our groom; tradition asks us not to neglect a good man's opinion, even if he is our father.[55]

No matter what generation I'm living in, this democracy of the dead called Historic Christian Orthodoxy is going to gut-punch me. The Scriptures are going to initially shock me: they serve as a cultural ice bath. But the consistency of the church in their readings on major points of doctrine will force me to a decision: Will I be a Christian, or will I be a "sorta Jesus guy"?

A Christian is someone who confesses the essential doctrines that the church has confessed for 1,500 years. A "sorta Jesus guy" is someone who is a man of his age and time, stuck in the feedback loop of modernity.

---

55. G. K. Chesterton, *Orthodoxy* (New York: John Lane Company, 1908), 85.

Christianity—according to him—is whatever is most politically palatable.

And living in New York City in 2022 is no excuse for being a self-deceived heretic.

I lived in the Big Apple for eight years, California for four years after that. Before New York I was in Portland, Oregon, for five years before that. I've lived in some progressive places.

I've become intimately acquainted with my generation's cultural leanings both in sharing the same space and in being on the internet and having thousands of exchanges.

I watch their news. I know their talking points. I've listened. I've listened intently.

I am one of them. But I'm not one of them.

I listen to the same music and watch the same movies and eat the same food and laugh at the same pop-culture jokes—but I might as well be an alien when it comes to my belief system.

I'm in but not of.

One of the things I noted as I attended and eventually came on staff at a large growing church in New York City for eight years was that the challenge wasn't to fill auditoriums but rather create Christians. Our church had a lot of people who were saved but weren't Christian.

They didn't think like Christians, they thought like New Yorkers living in 2022.

Everything they believed about God, the Bible, morality, worship, society, politics, others, and so on was not Christian; it was American, Western, Post-Modern,

Post-Christian, Liberal, Secular, and Metropolitan.

The task of the church for townies and country bumpkins alike is to create Christians, not Jesus-loving Democrats or Republicans.

In case you haven't noticed, I'm using the word "Christian" instead of "disciple" because I think "disciple" is an easily hijackable term—not that I'm against its use—but for the purposes of this chapter I'm sticking with "Christian" because of what comes with that term, baggage and all.

A Christian doesn't get to decide what they believe about hell or sin or sexuality: all of that is predetermined for them when they receive Jesus, because Jesus has words and His words are life, and if you reject His words you reject Him (John 14:15). And the church acts as a historic witness to the words of Christ as recorded in Scripture—particularly on essential doctrines.

When you become a Christian, you decide to trust Jesus, not your own understanding of Jesus.

Jesus is a historical person as documented by Scripture, and the church is a historical witness to the Scripture.

Within the great unity the church has had on the essentials of Christian doctrine (the Godhead, the Incarnation, Christology, sin and salvation, eternal states, etc.), there is lots of room for divergent methodological views on non-essentials (God's sovereignty, gender roles, the sacraments, church life, etc.).

But within the essentials of Historic Christian Orthodoxy, each generation of Christians are going to be challenged to be Christian or to become a product of their age.

One such stronghold in my generation is the concept of God being love.

God is love has become the most important herme-neutic of my generation: it is the lens by which everything in Scripture is adjudicated. And if any action in Scripture taken by God is not seen as "loving," then my generation has to come up with some dishonest way to explain away the action or embrace a more honest method that openly dismisses the troublesome passage as fake or lacking inspi-ration. This is a resurgence of the old Marcion heresy (the new heresies are just old heresies with new clothes).

The biggest problem is how we define love.

Does the Bible define love, or does our cultural bias inform love?

When we say "love" do we mean, "Just let them do what they want, man"?

Or do we mean, "If you love me, obey my com-mands," a direct quote from Jesus in John 14:15?

Where do we get this concept of love?

Because if "God is love" is your operating principle because "the Bible says God is love," you better make damn sure your theological concept of love is biblical too, lest you create God in your own cultural image.

LOVE IN THE BIBLE

The Christian concept of love comes from Scripture.

It begins with the Godhead—meaning, we look at how perfect love operates in the first eternal relationship, and then we work our way from there to other aspects. There's a hierarchy to this theological work, and we should start with how the Trinity exhibits love toward one another.

Another reason we will start with the Trinity and not a Greek word study is because Greek words have large semantic range and can mean different things in different contexts. For example, *agape* doesn't always mean "godly love." We know this because in the Septuagint, Amnon "agapes" his half-sister Tamar (you know, the one he lusted after and raped).[56]

We see first that the Father loves (*agapeo* John 3:35; *phileo* John 5:20) the Son, and the Son loves (*agapeo* John 14:31) the Father. In John 5:20, Jesus says, "For the Father loves the Son and shows him all that he himself is doing."

The way that the Father loves the Son is by showing Him the plan of redemption.

For whatever reason, I was raised by a father who loved to surprise us kids in everything: he loved telling the family to get ready because he was gonna take us some-where. It would drive my mother nuts.

Us kids loved it. Dad's surprises were always amaz-ing—rarely did they suck. Restaurants, hikes in the woods, trips to the batting cages, mini-golf—we loved it. And nat-urally we have this same bent toward surprising others.

But my wife—like my mother—doesn't want any of it. She wants to know the plan. And if she doesn't know the plan, she feels unloved. She wants to be included, and she feels love when she is included.

The Father loves the Son by including Him on the

---

56. For a study on exegetical fallacies, I recommend D. A. Carson, *Exegetical Fallacies, Second Edition* (Grand Rapids: Baker Books, 1996). We make all our Greek students at Theos Sem-inary read this work before handling the Greek text.

master plan of salvation history—this is what Jesus tells us.

Now, Jesus's love for the Father will be different because the Father is not the Son and the Son is not the Father—they are of the same substance but they are different persons with unique functions within the Trinity. The Father is the first among equals—His job is to come up with the plan; the Son is co-God, co-eternal and co-equal—yet there exists a diversity of function.

The Father loves the Son by telling Him the plan; the Son loves the Father by obeying the plan.

We see this outlined in John 14:31, where Jesus says, "I do as the Father has commanded me, so that the world may know that I love the Father."

In John 15:9–10, Jesus says to His disciples, "As the Father has loved me, so have I loved you. Abide in my love. If you keep my commandments, you will abide in my love, just as I have kept my Father's commandments and abide in his love."

The Father loves the Son by telling Him the plan; the Son loves the Father by obeying the plan. Jesus loves us by telling us the plan; we love Jesus by obeying the plan, just as Jesus has loved the Father by obeying the plan.

Are you seeing this?

"Love" in the Trinity is not based on how cute everyone is.

God is not a desperate boyfriend always slipping into your DMs, stalking you online, and kissing a poster of you that's tacked onto his bedroom wall.

"Love" in the Godhead is *ordered and* it is *conditional*.

Jesus pays this idea forward and places conditions on the disciples' ability to "abide in his love."

This is the highest form of love in Scripture.

We also see how God loves His creation, calling it "good" in Genesis 1; we even see how God providentially loves grass in Matthew 6. God cares about grass—how much more does He care for you? God cares about flowers that don't spin or toil—they don't do good works or "abide"—they just exist, but He cares for them.

This is a different kind of love—a *providential love*.

We also see God's love toward the big bad world in John 3:16: in the book of John, the use of "world"[57] is always pejorative. God stands in judgment of the world while at the same time He invites the world to repent and receive His love.

Next, we see how love is demonstrated by Jesus toward the church, His body (Eph. 5:25). Jesus died for the church, He laid down His life for the church. This is an example of *sacrificial love*, a love that husbands are commanded to exhibit toward their wives.

Then we see examples of a *provisional love*—a love that manifests itself uniquely based on our obedience (Jude 21; John 15:9–10; Ps. 103:9–11, 13, 17–18).

I always knew my dad loved me, even when I was getting the belt across my butt. His love manifested itself uniquely: sometimes it was in delight and reward, sometimes it was in disapproval and discipline. The choice was mine.

---

57. Carson confirms. He notes, "The 'world' in John's usage comprises no believers at all. Those who come to faith are no longer of this world; they have been chosen out of this world." See D. A. Carson, *The Gospel According to John* (Grand Rapids: Eerdmans, 1991), 123.

In John 5, Jesus says, "You are my friends if you obey my commands." We don't turn around and say, "And You can be *my friend* if You do what I want, Jesus." Jesus is my King and Lord. There is an order to His love.

In light of Scripture, we can easily state, "God's love is conditional: there are conditions to my remaining in His love: I must obey Him."

GOD IS HOLY

A concept that we seem to have lost altogether is the idea that God is holy, and this seems to be at odds with the idea that He is love.

God is called "holy" over 400 times in the Bible, from Genesis to Revelation.

In the New Testament, Jesus calls the Father, "Holy Father" (John 17:11).

The demons call Jesus, "Holy One of God" (Mark 1:24).

The third person of the Trinity's first name is "Holy."

He's not called Love Spirit; He's called Holy Spirit.

In Revelation 4:8, we get this incredible snapshot of heaven. John sees this throne room activity and records it, "And the four living creatures, each of them with six wings, are full of eyes all around and within, and day and night they never cease to say, 'Holy, holy, holy, is the Lord God Almighty, who was and is and is to come!'"

This gnarly band of freaky-looking rockstars—right out of a KISS or Alice Cooper show—circle the throne of God, and sing the same song all day and all night, never ceasing to say, "Holy, holy, holy, is the Lord God Almighty, who was and is and is to come!"

When these guys wrote the original Song That Never Ends, they had to be choosy about the lyrics, because they are describing YHWH—God Almighty—the Eternal One. It's important to note that they landed on "Holy" as the big idea—the chief descriptor—of their song.

Their song doesn't go, "Love, Love, Love."

That's the other Fab Four.

No, these fantastic beasts sing, "Holy, Holy, Holy,"

That is what the closest people to God right now are singing to Him.

Right now as you read this book, The Song That Never Ends goes on and on and on.

And "holy" is the word they continually employ.

Now, God is love.

The Bible says so.

Twice.

In the same passage.

But you would think—by the way my generation drones on and on about God's love—that all of this was the inverse. That the Bible says that God is love over 400 times, and that Jesus calls the Father "Loving Father," and the demons call Jesus the Loving One of God, and that the Holy Spirit's first name is Love, and that the song of heaven is Love, Love, Love.

It really feels that way in our songs and sermons and emphases and Instagram highlights and pithy Twitter sayings and critiques of church and modern theological musings: the overwhelming Christian truth of our culture is that God is love, and the overwhelming cultural definition of that word—even in the mouths of Christians—is that . . .

- God's love is unconditional, and
- God's love means grace, and
- God's love means He loves me just the way that I am and I don't need to change, and
- God's love is the message of the gospel and that means I don't need to repent, and
- holiness and the commandments of Christ and obeying God and all of that other stuff is peripheral and confusing and unclear and should be shoved in a closet, and
- the giant obvious idea of the Bible and the person of Jesus is love.

And what I'm suggesting today is this is a giant cultural lie.

And the bigger problem is that this is how we think of God: we think of Him as a desperate boyfriend and ourselves as this sad little victim on whom He takes pity because He's so empathetic.

The way we think about God matters because it informs our worship.

And as we take a long hard look at Scripture, we find this is not an accurate description of the God of the Bible: it's not how past generations of Christians would summarize their witness to Scripture or the workings of God throughout church history.

God is love, yes.

But God's love is a holy love.

It flows from His prior commitment to His absolute moral perfection.

God cannot and will not be unholy. He is totally and completely holy.

Because God is Holy, He is Love.

God will not violate His holiness for any reason. The entire story of the Old Testament is a holy God who loves His creation desiring to draw near to His creation, but the lingering reality of sin being an obstacle that He must deal with.

God didn't create sin, but sin came into the world because God's creation rebelled.

God initiated relationship with fallen creation even after their rebellion, but in order for humanity to fully appreciate who He is (for our benefit), we had to understand who we are, patricianly in relation to who God is.

The Scriptures are the story of Him and us.

It's a journey of God-discovery and self-discovery: humanity is collectively learning about who He is and who we are.

The Old Testament, then, develops this really important core concept about God: He is holy. He is different than us in that He is perfect, and is always perfect, and this perfection sets Him above creatures who have rebelled and inherited a sinful world.

In spite of sin, God reveals Himself but allows the rebellion to be a teaching moment. He will instruct us on sin, the scope of sin, the damage it causes, and God's solutions for it. God will be honored and seen in His proper place: far above sin yet coming into the sinful story to fix sin once and for good. He is a humble God who somehow maintains total holiness while being incarnated as a human male. He doesn't run away from us but draws near.

We appreciate the incarnation story because it is in light of the fundamental development of the problem and scope of sin as seen in the Old Testament: God's Presence is destructive to sinful people. But He will veil yet unveil (a paradox) His glory in the human form of Jesus Christ.

We will look upon this form of God and not die; we will be near Him and live.

This paradox of holiness and love in human form is tortured by the Romans unjustly, but according to the purposes of God. The death sentence ends up accomplishing a great many things as Jesus the Messiah hangs onto the instrument of His death.

What kept Jesus hanging onto His death?

Ultimately, the purpose of God to redeem humanity.

But if we boil down the theology of Paul, I see two major reasons for Jesus to stay on that cross: to satisfy the holiness of God, and to satisfy the love of God. The perfection of the Law had to be dealt with so that the love of God could be fully experienced by those of us that have put our faith in Jesus Christ.

Because of the blood of Jesus, my sins have been atoned for and thus removed; I have become the righteousness of God in Christ Jesus. I can boldly approach the throne of grace now that my sins have been removed by Jesus. Before, I could not approach God because of my sins, lest I perish from His holiness; God—having dealt with the righteous requirement of the Law—can allow me to approach Him in holiness. Holiness still matters to God—if it did not, Jesus wouldn't have died.

God loved the big bad world—He wanted it to be saved—and so He suffered on behalf of the world so the world could believe in Him and receive everlasting life.

Those that reject the suffering of God reject God's dealing with sin and thus are left with their sins, and the wrath of God remains on them.

THE PASSION: WHO YOU REALLY ARE

I love psychometrics[58]—I'm a huge fan. And to be honest, I like all of them. I love taking those personality tests and discovering what I'm like—probably because I'm so interested in me.

I've done the Meyers-Briggs assessment; I've taken the Enneagram test like ten times—my wife is obsessed. I've even followed these Enneagram accounts that tell you all about your numbers and wings, etc.

I even love finding out which Disney Princess I am on Facebook.

"Oh, Jasmine again—I do love a carpet ride."

But as my friend Jim McNeish always says, "That's not the truth about you. You aren't your trauma; you are your *passion*—what you are willing to suffer for. That's

---

58. Psychometrics is simply psychological measurement. In includes measuring and analyzing our own psychology and behaviorisms.

the truth about you."

As Jim explains, the word "passion" is a Latin word that means "to suffer."

When I want to know what God is like—what the truth about Him is—I can look to the great paradox that is the cross, where we see this incredible tension of two giant truths. On one hand we have His holiness—this mega revelation that doesn't stop unfolding in Scripture—and on the other hand His Love, an essential attribute of His that is proven over and over again canonically.

God is holy and God is love.

And on the cross—in the Passion of Christ—we see God truly because we see what He was willing to suffer for.

He suffered for His holiness, and He suffered for His love.

He would not compromise either.

And a mature believer is invited to pick up both of these seemingly contradictory realities in Scripture. Rather than throwing one out because of our cultural conditioning—in the case of my grandmother, God's love; and in the case of my generation, God's holiness—we are called as Christians to do as Christians have done for two millennia: to allow both of these things to be true.

An overemphasis on the holiness of God leads to legalism and a merit-based theology.

An overemphasis on the love of God leads to a licentiousness and self-absorbed theology.

An overemphasis on the holiness of God in our ecclesiology leads to a neglect of sinners.

An overemphasis on the love of God in our ecclesiology leads to a neglect of the saints.

God is holy and love, and yet there is still an order:
God's love is a Holy Love.

That's what God is like.

Chapter Eight

CHRISTIAN BUDDHISM

I was recently watching a show called *Botched* on the Discovery Channel. It's one of those series that are like a fiery car wreck on the interstate: you can't look away. You pump the brakes and slow down and become embroiled in the carnage.

Botched is about people who have suffered malpractice at the hands of idiot cosmetic surgeons, whose lives have been a horror as they walk around like freak shows.

Breast implants that have punctured or leaked, nose jobs that have fallen apart, liposuction that has left people lopsided, lip injections that have collapsed, and tummy tucks that resemble a Gettysburg battlefield surgery: the stories are horrific. These poor people had hopes of being better, and a foolish doctor ruined their lives. Now they come to the best cosmetic surgeons in LA to have their self-esteem repaired.

Often when I'm watching TV it's because I'm about

to go to bed and it just numbs the cares of the day: TV doesn't stir me up, it calms me down. I put on half a show of *American Pickers* or *Southpark* and I'm out.

But this show revved me up: it actually brought something to the surface in me that I didn't even realize was there. And that is this: I don't trust professionals.

I've been familiar with the crisis of authority for a long time now: I know the basic historical facts—that we no longer trust priests and kings because of abuses as well as the advent of science and democracy. I know that the creation of the individual and the accomplishments and prioritization of the individual in Western society have been remarkable.

And I also know about the great weight that rests on the individual: if you can't trust priests, kings, and what the Bible says, that's a great deal of pressure. Education isn't an option in a society with this much pressure: everyone has to be their very best self!

But then when you add into the mix the reality of malpractice: that individuals who have come up through our seemingly reliable education systems, have passed exams, have obtained licenses, and perhaps have done good work in the past, can just operate on you and ruin your life? . . . well that's really scary.

One of my best friend's dad died a couple months ago. He went in for a routine operation to get screws taken out of his knee from a previous operation. He bled out on the operating table.

The family is still in shock.

It was routine.

He didn't even tell half of them he was going in.

Mechanics mess up cars.

Carpenters mess up flooring.

Doctors mess up people.

Presidents mess up countries.

Judges mess up decisions.

There's a crisis of authority.

I remember my friend recently telling me about how he started to do a ton of research when his wife got cancer. He was telling me that he became an expert in the type of cancer she had. He studied all the best therapies, the best hospitals for those therapies—he knew all of the language for the procedures around these therapies—I was bewildered.

I remember thinking, *Why?*

Now I know "why": because there is a crisis of authority.

We don't trust doctors because not every doctor is the same: they aren't all committed to the craft as others are. There are good ones and there are average ones and there are bad ones. There are disinterested ones who don't care about new ways to fight cancer; there are detached ones who are thinking about golf; and there are negligent ones who cut corners and take needless risks.

There are PhDs who propagate horrible theology.

Because of this crisis of authority, we are forced to become experts at things we are not experts at. We feel compelled to scour the internet in an attempt to find reliable sources. We have to mull through countless customer reviews, deciphering between the paid bots and the actual human experiences in hopes of making the right purchase or booking the right trip.

When we find another person who has had a great experience and swears by a product or experience, our heart jumps: we've found something we can rely on.

This crisis of authority consumes us.

And it permeates culture.

Career Christians have to understand that new people who are investigating Christianity or a potential church are operating under a crisis of authority unseen in generations past.

The crisis of authority has ramped up to peak levels of late: this is where the obsession with self-development comes in. Seeing that we cannot trust external forms of authority, we must become the greatest versions of ourselves possible. The locus of interpretation rests on the self.

This is why psychometrics are particularly so appealing: we are trying to answer questions far more nuanced than previous.

And seeing that Jungian psychotherapy[59] has taught us that we are basically the result of trauma, spiritual or emotional healing is king. If we can just not be led around by our basic instincts or pain, we can actually operate out of peace and thus make the right decisions all of the time, or so the idea goes.

Having achieved super-galactic omni-oneness after radically accepting our past, gazing non-judgmentally at the tangled tinsel that is our self-consciousness, and

---

59. For an introduction to Jung, see C. G. Jung, *Introduction to Jungian Psychology: Notes of the Seminar on Analytical Psychology Given in 1923* (Princeton, NJ: Princeton University Press, 2012).

coming to terms with the deck of cards that we've been given, somehow we become the highest form of ourselves and can discover and know truth—or that is the belief.

Forms of spirituality that promote radical acceptance of self, self-love, love vibes in general, and a connection to the Divine are optimal for your average millennial who is just trying to self-discover, achieve this higher state of consciousness, and heal.

And this is why Christianity is so wildly popular among spiritualists.

Because we talk about love a lot.

And being accepted by God.

And loved by God.

And healed by God.

And we've got good vibes—earthy, spiritual, self-accepting vibes.

We cry at church. We breathe the air. We have moments of relaxing calm in our worship sets.

And we look so cool now too.

Oh, and we don't talk about sin or rebellion or wrath; we sing about how we are broken, like we're victims—victims of trauma, like our childhood-wounding archetypes. We don't preach the cross or self-denial as a way of life or a call; we talk about relationships, which are actually the highest form of spirituality.

Because eros (mutual infatuation) is the highest spiritual experience available in the West.

When love for God, King, and Country were done away with at the turn of the twentieth century, a massive hole began to develop in the hearts of modern people—and eros (mutual infatuation) began to occupy that space. You see it in the entire arc of narrative in the 1900s: before the 1900s, impulsive eros was almost always seen as tragic—the Russians particularly noted this. But at the turn of the century, as the heart no longer had traditional meta-narratives to fill it, eros began to ravage it. The stories of Hollywood depict the cultural shift. Eros normalized divorce in the '30s and '40s; it sexualized the work office and music in the '50s; it was engrained in youth culture in the '60s and '70s; and it crescendoed in the spread of disease and pregnancy in the '80s—even documented in pop films like *Forrest Gump*.

Eros mutated into identity in the '90s and 2000s.

And now it seeks to groom kindergarteners without their parents' permission.

We are obsessed with sex.

Our relationships keep breaking down because we think eros is the fundamental brick, the end, the telos, what makes us alive.

That's what Disney told us: true love's kiss makes us come alive.

If we can't be in love, then we must leave family and friends and run away, because I am a priestess of Aphrodite, and if she is not worshipped, I don't feel alive.

Shakespeare called that a tragedy—his message has gone sailing over our heads.

I digress. What is my point? Many times our churches cater to spiritualists and temple prostitutes.

Now, let's define Christian Buddhism in light of this diatribe.

Christian Buddhism is the Christ of the modern church on our terms for the purpose of meeting our cultural needs: it is spirituality that is detached from authority, for the purpose of self-authority, or to use a popular modern term, self-authoring.

Jesus doesn't write my story; I write my story: Jesus is peripheral to my story because I am at the center of it. And I add Him into my life as need be.

God is on their side, we tell them.

They are blessed, we tell them.

They desire the divine impartation of peace, hope, love, and faith—for their purposes.

Faith, to the Christian Buddhist, is simply "manifestation."

Christian Buddhists love the "faith message" because it has nothing to do with the God of the Bible or what He wants—particularly the way it's oft presented. Faith isn't taught as a response to the word of Christ, but rather as a presumption upon God's will.

"I think I have a God dream (presumption). This will make me happy and it's not a *bad* thing, so if I just have faith for it, it will happen. I love this church."

This typical takeaway carries zero resemblance to the faith of the Bible.

Now, a Seeker and a Christian Buddhist are not the same. A Seeker is someone who is thirsty, and has a sense of humility; they need God deep in their soul and they know it. A seeker recognizes the power of sin over their life and sees the gospel as the power of God unto salvation. A Christian Buddhist doesn't believe in the biblical scope of sin, because ultimately they don't believe there is anything really wrong with themselves. Yes, they need some vibes and healing to be a better person, but they don't need God. They *are* god.

They don't need to be saved; they need their spiritual needs met.

The crisis of authority puts the Christian Buddhist in the driver's seat; it's also what brought them to your church—they are on a spiritual journey and they've decided that the vibes you create are beneficial for them; if you attempt to disciple them, they will leave in a huff. If you continue to create positive vibes and generic "God loves you" atmospheres, they will continue to attend your church.

The great challenge in ministering to Christian Buddhists is establishing that Scripture is the ultimate authority, that Jesus and His words cannot be separated. This violates everything that they believe about reality: their entire framework has to be thrown out in order to accept that someone else has all authority, and that they must submit *their entire life* to this person.

But they will become increasingly disillusioned and eventually quite spiritually ill if they continue to attempt to use Jesus in this way—and the only one to blame will be our churches.

Because our churches don't heal Christian Buddhists—they make them sicker.

They were designed that way.

Chapter Nine

BROTHERS IN DANGEROUS TIMES

I have two nieces, Francesca and Georgiana. They are my sister's kids and they are the light of my life. Frankie is six and Georgie is three.

Frankie is a tomboy; she's always wearing spandex so she can roundhouse kick you to the face. She loves watching *Ninja Kids* on YouTube, destroying stuff, and choking out her younger sister.

Georgie is a girly-girl; she's obsessed with Barbies and Disney Princesses. She's always getting her nails painted and she wouldn't be caught dead in spandex. Georgie only wears dresses—princess dresses.

Georgie's big rule on her dresses is that they have to *swirl*. Every time she puts on a dress, she stands in front of a long mirror and spins around, to see if the dress swirls. If it doesn't swirl enough, she finds another one.

I was FaceTiming my mum and sister last summer and the girls had just returned from a day of shopping at thrift stores. My mother is a brilliant seamstress, and my sister bought a ton of dresses for Georgie that were too big but could be adjusted.

My sister was holding the phone and showed me Georgie in a big dress, my mum on her knees putting pins in the fabric as markers for where the dress needed to be hemmed. Mum finished her work and said to Georgie, "Okay, Georgie, twirl! Show Uncle Nate!"

Georgie tried to twirl but there was too much material bunched up by the pins, and so the dress wouldn't spin.

She started to bawl her eyes out.

"Quick!" Mum shouted. "Take it off her, take it off her!"

My sister lifted the dress over her head and quickly pulled her familiar dress back over her head. She immediately stopped crying and did a swirl.

Phew . . .

When I read the Cain and Abel story in Genesis 4, I can't help but see Georgie in Cain.

Cain and Abel are brothers and in Genesis 4 we see them at the first worship service ever recorded in Scripture. Cain brings "an offering," whereas Abel brings "the firstborn of his flock" and "fatty portions," which is ancient Near Eastern speak for "the good stuff."[60]

Meaning, Cain mailed his worship in, but Abel brought a thoughtful and costly gift. There was priority in Abel's gift to God—his heart was in it and that showed in the extravagance of the gift. But Cain's heart wasn't in it.

God accepted Abel's offering, but for Cain's offering "he had no regard."

---

60. See Genesis 4:1–5.

As in, God didn't want Cain's leftovers—or a tip. God wanted to be revered and treated as God—as someone important that is honored.

When Cain saw that his offering was rejected, he became jealous of Abel and killed him.

The dress didn't swirl, and so he got sad.

It was all about Cain and how he wants life to be. Cain didn't give a rip about anyone else but himself—a truth so evident that he kills his own brother because he doesn't get what he wants.

Old Testament scholar Bruce Waltke notes, "Cain's failure at the altar leads to his failure in the field: theology and ethics are inseparable."[61]

But I think there is something else at play here; there is a power that Cain is warned about by God that Cain must resist (Gen. 4:7). And Cain's failure to resist the power of sin and self-absorption brought death in the field.

Cain's failure in worship brought death—not just to Abel, but to himself. His life takes a turn for the worst in the murder of Abel.

It was at the altar that Cain had an opportunity to trust God—to show God consciousness—and in doing so to reduce the power of sin over his life. Sin is lurking at Cain's door, desiring to become his master, and to dictate how he will view God and others. Sin wants Cain to be self-reliant and self-authoring.

In treating God with contempt at the altar, Cain was giving into sin: his pathetic offering to God was an

---

61. Bruce Waltke, *An Old Testament Theology: An Exegetical, Canonical, and Thematic Approach* (Grand Rapids: Zondervan, 2007), 27.

outward manifestation of his distrust for God internally. Abel's offering was his best because he recognized his need. Cain has no need, therefore he worships like it.

His worship directly reflects the state of his faith.

The result is death and more death—a detachment from God.

God is still merciful, marking Cain with a protective seal. But in his punishment, Cain is still thinking about himself. He isn't sorry about Abel—he's sorry that his journey has taken a turn for the worst.

Cain is a Christian Buddhist.

When he worships God his way rather than God's way, it doesn't work because God doesn't accept the worship of self-absorbed spiritualists. He resists the proud.

It would have been better if Cain had not worshipped at all than to have worshipped in this way.

BROTHERS FROM ANOTHER MOTHER

Fast-forwarding from Genesis we get to Leviticus, where another pair of brothers are about to have their first worship service as priests.

Things are a little different: YHWH has shown up and revealed Himself in a more robust way to Moses, instituting an entire sacrificial system and priesthood. YHWH wants to be in relationship with people but He doesn't want repeats of the Cain incident, so He gets meticulous. He tells Moses what He likes and what He doesn't like.

He tells Moses about the avocado toast—what His preferences are.

Moses has God's acceptable forms of worship nailed down to a *T*.

Next, Moses ordains a priesthood. It's a long, gaudy process—there are exact types of robes and exact types of materials to be used for those robes, and there are exact types of protocol for using the instruments of the tabernacle. Everything is very particular and orderly, just the way YHWH wants things to be.

And this is a good trade because YHWH is Israel's God and blessed them with His Presence and goodness—all the details of worship are worth hosting YHWH's glory in Israel.

In Leviticus 10 we find Nadab and Abihu—sons of Aaron the high priest—about to worship as priests for the first time. They've undergone an ordination ritual involving blood sprinkling: the blood of ordination is still drying on their big right toe and right thumb and right ear lobe. They've got their special robes on—they're feeling pretty priestly. They've just dined with God months earlier, beholding YHWH's glory. You could say these guys are on a high.

What happens next is insane: they fill their censers with fire that God had not asked for—essentially presuming that YHWH was down with any kind of worship protocol that Nadab and Abihu thought appropriate.

Leviticus 10:1–3 (NIV) reads:

> Aaron's sons Nadab and Abihu took their
> censers, put fire in them and added incense;
> and they offered unauthorized fire before

the LORD, contrary to his command. So fire came out from the presence of the LORD and consumed them, and they died before the LORD. Moses then said to Aaron, "This is what the LORD spoke of when he said:

> "'Among those who approach me
>   I will be proved holy;
> in the sight of all the people
>   I will be honored.'"

Aaron remained silent.

They offered fire "contrary to his command," and *boom*—they're fried crispy.

More deaths at a worship service.

Moses then explains what happened with YHWH's own words: "Among those who approach me, I will be proved holy; in the sight of all the people I will be honored" (v. 3).

By "holy," YHWH means, "I'm separate—I'm special. I'm not a cow or a tree that you can just come up to and pat. I'm a powerful unique person and I want to be thought of as such. And you need to think of me as such."[62]

YHWH also says that He wants to be honored in the sight of the people, meaning that Israel has to figure out that YHWH is a real-life King, and He should be revered and awed as someone whose Presence is special and appreciated and admired.

---

62. In Leviticus 10:3, the Hebrew word is *qdš*. It means "to be set apart, consecrated, hallowed." See *Brown-Driver-Briggs Hebrew and English Lexicon* (Peabody, MA: Hendrickson, 1996), 872–73.

Nadab and Abihu thought that there was something special about themselves, since YHWH had invited them to dinner (Exod. 24:1–18) and gifted them the priesthood. This is why they presumed, assumed, and speculated upon YHWH's mode of worship: it was a blatant act of self-absorption.

There was zero God-consciousness and thus self-consciousness in this act.

What I mean by that is, as I know God, I am able to have an accurate estimation of myself. Here's a pithy little axiom to live by: there is a God, and I am not Him.

I'm not holy, God is.

If I am welcomed into His friendship, it is because God is gracious and wonderful and merciful and kind and loving. And I should treasure this welcome with wonder and thankfulness and awe.

I recall how my parents used to prep my brother and I for a visit to someone else's home—I remember it like yesterday, because of how clear and emphatic their warnings were.

"Stay off the furniture; don't touch the walls; no running; be polite; no horseplay."

For a stranger, who is an equal, we're asked to show respect.

If my brother and I obeyed, things would go well; if we disobeyed and were rambunctious, we would be severely disciplined.

But in Leviticus 10, the stakes are higher. This is the institution of the Levitical system and its laws. YHWH can't let this one slide: He has to be seen as holy and honored among the people. Nadab and Abihu are elected, called to the priesthood, welcomed to YHWH's table, yet somehow in all of this—rather than being humbled and thankful for the opportunity—they are filled with hubris and treat the opportunity so cavalierly.

Their failure at the altar leads to death.

Chapter Ten

A TALE OF TWO KINGS

My niece Georgie is a chocolate and Krispy Kreme junkie.

"Uncle Nate, I need some gockwick."

"I know, buddy, me too, but Mummy said no gockwick today."

She loves pink glazed doughnuts with rainbow sprinkles. She'll do a deep voice—like she's possessed by a legion—and eerily shout, "Douuuuughnuuuuts!"

Georgie doesn't know me—she doesn't have a clue who I am or what I'm like or what I like—for all she knows I'm Willy Wonka. I'm just her sugar dealer. She has zero interest in finding out who I am or even some really good uncle tips.

She bristles when I tell her that chocolate and doughnuts aren't good to eat all the time.

Georgie wants what Georgie wants—twirling dresses, sprinkled doughnuts, and creamy chocolates—and she will freak out if life doesn't lead down that path.

At the age of three, it's cute and hilarious and mildly irritating but mostly tolerable. Having in mind the end goal of a responsible adult who stewards her life well, who shows interest in God and others, and lives for things beyond her instant gratification, it's fairly easy to look past her momentary immaturity.

But Georgie could become a spiritual version of her physical self. A dualism could take root in her life that leads her down a path of physical fruitfulness but spiritual barrenness. And the truth is that when spiritual things are bad, they begin to leak into physical things. As Paul the apostle noted, "for while bodily training is of some value, godliness is of value in every way, as it holds promise for the present life and also for the life to come" (1 Tim. 4:8).

Spiritual health leaks into our present life in a more impactful way than physical health.

So many Christians approach God and the church like Georgie—in their Christian Buddhist lean—trying to baptize their idolatry at every turn.

God isn't put off by immature Christians, but the journey is toward spiritual maturity. And these warnings from the Old Testament that we mentioned in the last chapter are the truth: Christianity is not about you; it's about God and others.

And so we need to speak "the truth in love [so that we] may grow up in all things into Him who is the head"—growing up into the image of Jesus Christ (Eph. 4:15 NKJV).

"Well that's cool, Nate, but God looks at the heart, not

just empty forms. And my intentions are good."

What if I told you that the forms reveal the heart, and your good intentions sometimes don't matter?

KING DAVID AND UZZAH

In 2 Samuel 6 and 1 Chronicles 13, we find this insane story about King David. As we noted earlier, King David was obsessed with the Presence of God. In this story, we find him bringing the ark of God into Jerusalem after it had been recaptured from the Philistines, who had taken it in war decades earlier.

David throws this massive city-wide worship party and puts this massive musical production together: "David and all the Israelites were celebrating with all their might before God, with songs and with harps, lyres, timbrels, cymbals and trumpets" (1 Chron. 13:8).

"All their might" stands out to me. They aren't lifting their hands for five seconds during the last chorus of "Good Good Father" while thinking about lunch. This crowd is going hard; the noise fills the city streets; the passion is tangible.

And everything looks good so far: they've got the worship team, their hearts are on fire, they are doing this before the Lord and for Him.

But these beautiful elements of sincere enthusiasm and exuberance in the pot of worship are overpowered and soured by some other problematic ingredients: a total disregard for YHWH's self-revelation.

Uzzah, a priest, has presumed that YHWH wouldn't

mind riding on a wooden cart pulled by two oxen—the ancient Near East equivalent of the back of an unsteady pickup truck. Being that Uzzah is a priest, it's his job to know the Mosaic protocol: priests are people who mediate between YHWH and the people. He's supposed to be advising this whole shindig, making sure that God is honored to the max.

But he's a lousy priest. David is partly to blame too: it is the king's job to have a copy of the book of the Law (Deut. 17:18), and to know the book of the Law so that all of Israel's interactions with YHWH are to code. First Chronicles 13:9–10 (NIV) reads:

> When they came to the threshing floor of Kidon, Uzzah reached out his hand to steady the ark, because the oxen stumbled. The LORD's anger burned against Uzzah, and he struck him down because he had put his hand on the ark. So he died there before God.

Our gut reaction might be, "Why would God kill someone? He was just trying to stop the ark from tipping over."

But we have to look at this from God's view: Why the hell is He riding in the back of a pickup truck? It's the ark of the covenant—a giant box covered with gold that is the dwelling place of God on earth—it's the most important piece of furniture on the planet because it is the throne of God!

And all God has asked is that the ark be carried by the

priests. It's not crazy difficult, He just wants the respect that Israel would show a Sovereign—a Great King. YHWH is God—He's to be worshipped and honored—He's not your nephew visiting from out of town that you make sit in the back. He's not a dog that He should be relegated to the back of the pickup truck.

I wouldn't even put a TV that I cared about, much less the ark of the covenant, in the back of a pickup truck.

Have you ever seen those goobers that try to strap down a mattress and twelve other household items to the back of their truck with bungee cords? I saw a guy the other day lose a box with all his albums from the back of his truck—the entire Beatles discography was spread across I-10. And you're thinking to yourself, *What is this animal doing? How did he think that would remotely work?*

This is how we need to see the Uzzah incident: Uzzah is checked out and frankly, so is David.

David is operating in his comfort zone—his sweet spot. He's awesome at the Cecil B. DeMille scale of production: David doesn't spare the horses when He's worshipping God, but problematically, if it's not God's way, it's not honoring.

And this worship service without truth has become a spectacle—a smoking spectacle—because Uzzah just got fried and the worship service has come to an abrupt end.

Two chapters later, we catch up with David—who has had a long hard think about this worship failure. He's probably picked up from perusing the Torah that deaths at worship services are a theme, and now he's part of the casualty list. David knows what to do know, and so he's going to re-attempt an ark retrieval. The Chronicler records David's thoughts:

> Then David summoned Zadok and Abiathar the priests, and Uriel, Asaiah, Joel, Shemaiah, Eliel and Amminadab the Levites. He said to them, "You are the heads of the Levitical families; you and your fellow Levites are to consecrate yourselves and bring up the ark of the LORD, the God of Israel, to the place I have prepared for it. It was because you, the Levites, did not bring it up the first time that the LORD our God broke out in anger against us. We did not inquire of him about how to do it in the prescribed way." So the priests and Levites consecrated themselves in order to bring up the ark of the LORD, the God of Israel. And the Levites carried the ark of God with the poles on their shoulders, as Moses had commanded in accordance with the word of the LORD. (1 Chron. 15:11–15)

This time they will do things exactly how God wants things to be done.

What amazes me is the confidence that David now has in worship. It is in this second movement of the ark into Jerusalem that David will dance with a linen ephod—a garment only the priests were to wear. The lines that David will cross will not be ones that dishonor YHWH, but they will be lines that bring Him closer to YHWH: David is not a Levite but he will dress as a Levite because he sees himself in the way that God actually wants all of Israel to see themselves: as a nation of priests.

And his wife Michal will look down upon him in disgust as he dances before the Lord. Second Samuel 6:20–23 reads:

> But Michal the daughter of Saul came out to meet David and said, "How the king of Israel honored himself today, uncovering himself today before the eyes of his servants' female servants, as one of the vulgar fellows shamelessly uncovers himself!" And David said to Michal, "It was before the LORD, who chose me above your father and above all his house, to appoint me as prince over Israel, the people of the LORD—and I will celebrate before the LORD. I will make myself yet more contemptible than this, and I will be abased in your eyes. But by the female servants of whom you have spoken, by them I shall be held in honor." And Michal the daughter of Saul had no child to the day of her death.

David is emboldened by YHWH worship that is in truth and he dances with nothing but a linen ephod on— without all his rich luxurious robes—because he's breaking a sweat dancing before the Lord. The truth is a jungle gym, and David is swinging from the bars.

Worship is not about David or how he may be perceived, but about being present in glory—giving YHWH *chabad*, no matter what people think—and this is why David's throne will be established forever; He is a man after God's heart.

David doesn't care what people think about him; he seeks to please YHWH.

Michal ridicules the altar and receives death by it.

KING UZZIAH AND ISAIAH

King Uzziah is one of the greatest kings of Judah and, like Saul, had an incredible start. He absolutely mangled his enemies and reinforced the borders of Israel against their political rivals. Second Chronicles 26:4–5 says that he did what was right in the eyes of the Lord, and as long as sought the Lord, he prospered. When you read through the book of Kings and Chronicles, you understand that this is high praise, all things considered.

Most of the kings of the Northern Kingdom of Israel were evil; around half of the kings of Judah were good, half were bad. God used other nations to judge Israel and Judah whenever they strayed from Him.

Uzziah's military victories were a direct result, then, of God's favor.

Second Chronicles 26:15 (NIV) says that he invented weapons similar to trebuchets and large bows for wall defenses: He was "greatly helped, until he became powerful."

But this is when things began to go downhill for him, because "pride goeth before a fall."[63]

The Chronicler tells us this sobering story—more death at a worship service:

> But after Uzziah became powerful, his pride led to his downfall. He was unfaithful to the LORD his God, and entered the temple of the LORD to burn incense on the altar of incense. Azariah the priest with eighty other courageous priests of the LORD followed him in. They confronted King Uzziah and said, "It is not right for you, Uzziah, to burn incense to the LORD. That is for the priests, the descendants of Aaron, who have been consecrated to burn incense. Leave the sanctuary, for you have been unfaithful; and you will not be honored by the LORD God."
>
> Uzziah, who had a censer in his hand ready to burn incense, became angry. While he was raging at the priests in their presence before the incense altar in the LORD's temple, leprosy broke out on his forehead. When Azariah the chief priest and all the other priests looked at him, they saw that he had leprosy on his forehead, so they hurried him out. Indeed, he himself was eager

---

63. See Proverbs 16:18.

to leave, because the LORD had afflicted
him.

King Uzziah had leprosy until the day he
died. He lived in a separate house—lep-
rous, and banned from the temple of the
LORD. (2 Chron. 26:16–21 NIV)

Once again, a situation that may have been avoided
had King Uzziah read a copy of the Law of Moses. All
he'd need to do is read Leviticus 10 and realize that this
type of thing doesn't go down well.

It's crazy how the blessing of God can make you dan-
gerously proud. You start thinking that it's about you and
not about God's mercy; you start thinking that the world
revolves around you.

This is the same Uzziah that Isaiah the prophet talks
about in Isaiah 6:1–4 (NIV):

In the year that King Uzziah died, I saw the
Lord, high and exalted, seated on a throne;
and the train of his robe filled the temple.
Above him were seraphim, each with six
wings: With two wings they covered their
faces, with two they covered their feet, and
with two they were flying. And they were
calling to one another:

"Holy, holy, holy is the LORD
Almighty;

> the whole earth is full of his
> glory."

> At the sound of their voices the doorposts
> and thresholds shook and the temple was
> filled with smoke.

In the year that Uzziah died—the king that was so out of touch with reality that he presumed to offer incense in the holy place before the ark—Isaiah saw God.

In the Old Testament, when someone dies, a new revelation or word from God often comes. When Pharaoh died, God spoke to Moses; when Moses died, God spoke to Joshua. Sometimes it is significant. In the case of Isaiah, when we contrast these two stories, I think it is significant that Isaiah has this vision in the year King Uzziah dies from leprosy.

First, let's look at what Isaiah sees:

1. He sees the throne room of God.
2. He sees the four living creatures singing The Song That Never Ends.
3. He sees The Song That Never Ends shake the entire temple structure because it's such a powerful song and the band is obviously loud, pumping that bass.

Based on these things, Isaiah has a panic attack: "Woe to me! . . . I am ruined! For I am a man of unclean lips, and I live among a people of unclean lips, and my eyes have seen the King, the LORD Almighty" (Isa. 6:5 NIV).

After hearing The Song That Never Ends, and seeing God in His throne room, Isaiah has the exact opposite reaction as Uzziah. Uzziah has no revelation of God's holiness, enters the holy place (the temple of God), and presumes to stand before the Lord in his own holiness.

Isaiah sees the temple and starts shouting, "I'm in some deep crap, because I've got a potty mouth and I live with other potty mouths—and now I've just seen the King, the Lord Almighty."

Isaiah calls YHWH by the name used in the song—Almighty.

But this is where things get interesting: based off of Isaiah's freakout, where Isaiah sees the greatness of God and is overwhelmed by his sinfulness in relation to God's perfection, grace is extended. The passage continues:

> Then one of the seraphim flew to me with a live coal in his hand, which he had taken with tongs from the altar. With it he touched my mouth and said, "See, this has touched your lips; your guilt is taken away and your sin atoned for." (vv. 6–8 NIV)

- Isaiah confesses and is cleansed; Uzziah presumes and is made unclean.
- Isaiah humbles himself and is made holy; Uzziah elevates himself and is made unholy.
- Isaiah has a moment of self-consciousness and lives; Uzziah exhibits no self-consciousness and

dies.

- Isaiah sees the temple and is sanctified by the altar; Uzziah sees the temple and is condemned by the altar.
- Isaiah expects God's wrath and receives grace; Uzziah speculates upon God's grace and receives wrath.

When the Lord is the one who does the cleansing work, confidence in His cleansing work is the result; when I am the one trying to do the cleansing work, a lack of confidence is the result.

Isaiah is emboldened for greater worship as a result of the coal from the altar, the same effect that we see with David, who is emboldened for greater worship as a result of the confidence knowing that YHWH has been honored.

Isaiah says this after the cleansing in verse 8 (NIV):

> Then I heard the voice of the Lord saying,
> "Whom shall I send? And who will go for us?"
>
> And I said, "Here am I. Send me!"

One second ago this guy is an unwilling candidate—after the cleansing, he's a volunteer with his hand way up.

Revelation of God's ways brings faith and life; assumption of God's ways is a hubris that brings death.

Chapter Eleven

OUR PETS' HEADS ARE FALLING OFF

So we just read four scary stories about how people in the Old Testament are dying at worship services. And some of you are like, *Yeah, that's nuts, a bit sobering.*

But others of you are sitting there with your arms crossed and thinking, *I don't serve Old Testament God—I serve New Testament God—and He is obsessed with meh* (valley girl speak for "me").

You're thinking, *Okay, Nate, that's great, but I don't live under the Law anymore—I'm protected from the Law by Jesus. It's just all grace now. God doesn't judge Christians after the cross.*

Really?

I mean, you really wanna know the truth?

Because I'm gonna show you some Scriptures in the New Testament that will make you pee in your pants a little.

There are instances in the Testament when things are *no bueno*. There's turmoil. Down times. In the words of

Jerry Lee Lewis, *there's a whole lotta shakin' going on.*

Their situation makes me think of Lloyd Christmas and Harry Dunne, the two incompetent roommates from *Dumb and Dumber.* Things couldn't get any worse for the duo. They finally hit rock bottom when Harry's parakeet, Petey, dies. Lloyd comes into the apartment and finds Harry dismayed. Harry informs him of the bird's death and explains the cause of death: "his head fell off."

Lloyd snaps. He's HAD it.

He shouts, "We got no food! We no jobs! OUR PETS' HEADS ARE FALLING OFF!"

Whether you like it or not, heads fall off in the New Testament.

There are a lot of Christians out there who want you to think that Old Testament God is not the same as New Testament God. It's like the Bad Cop Good Cop shtick that we love in those interrogation room scenes in movies, where the first cop goes in and starts to beat the guy with a phone book. And that's the Father in our theological timeline: He's the one "throwing the book" at us, slamming four inches of paper against our cheekbone with two hands.

Then Jesus comes in, and He's the good cop. He pulls the Father off of us, lifts our chair back up, unlocks the handcuffs, and offers us a cigarette.

While these guys work out distinct functions of salvation history, they are working together and have the same mind and spirit. Jesus doesn't save us from the Father; He saves us from Him.

Jesus is YHWH.[64]

ANANIAS AND SAPHIRA

Without getting lost in the weeds—like whether God is ever retributive in His justice since the cross (He is)[65]—let's go straight into the first sobering passage that put the fear of God into the early church—the Ananias and Saphira narrative found in Acts 5.

To set the story up, Christians in Jerusalem are selling property in order to feed the starving persecuted church. Ananias and Saphira are believed to be Christians by most scholars,[66] are counted among the brethren in this passage, and are accused of lying to the Holy Spirit. People who don't have a relationship with the Spirit can't lie to the Spirit.

In any case, this couple thinks it's a good idea to sell their land, keep back a portion of the profits for themselves, and appear like pious "all in" Kingdom Builders, when really they are using the occasion to garner favor with their community in some sort of perverted sense.

They are essentially using tragedy to their advantage,

---

64. John 8:58, Jesus spells it right out here. The Greek "I AM" (*ego eimi*) is Christ's admission to deity and serves as a textual link to Isaiah 41:4 and Exodus 3:14, identifying Christ with YHWH. See D. A. Carson, *The Gospel According to John* (Grand Rapids: Eerdmans, 1991), 358 and Daniel. B. Wallace, *Greek Grammar Beyond the Basics* (Grand Rapids: Zondervan, 1996), 530–31.

65. Acts 12:23, this is after the cross and an angel kills Herod for not giving glory to God. The verse says that he was eaten by worms, in order to add an element of severity to the punishment. Keep in mind that Luke is including this in his report on the supernatural Christian church. How someone can read this and suggest that God in Christ is not retributive in His justice is beyond me.

66. David G. Peterson refers to this situation as a "serious internal conflict" and considers Ananias and Saphira to be "disciples." See David G. Peterson, *The Acts of the Apostles* (Grand Rapids: Eerdmans, 2009), 208–9.

but more importantly, they are hurting others by not sharing what God has given them. The situation is dire, and everyone must share or else some will perish.

It's a matter of life or death.

The Holy Spirit kills these folks (it is implied, they drop dead separately in front of Peter when they both lie about the money) for lying to the Spirit. It is possible that this happens because the concept of the Spirit is a relatively new one to the church, and the Holy Spirit is trying to underline that He is indeed God and the church has not been abandoned by Jesus but rather left in the most capable hands—God's hands.

The Holy Spirit is God.

So that may very well be the point of this passage, and the bigger point of their death, but it appears to me as a similar pattern to Leviticus 10. We are early on in the life of the church, and the Holy Spirit must be worshipped and honored and revered as God. Forms of worship are being instituted by a new priesthood, and just as Nadab and Abihu were consumed for their hubris at the ordination of the priests, now this couple have been consumed at the altar of the church—it is where they laid down their irreverential worship (at the feet of the apostles) that they died.

On a lighter note, I always wondered what the early church did with their bodies.

Good luck trying to convince the local police department that "God killed them."

Did they give them cement shoes and drop them into the Sea of Galilee, maffioso-style? Or did they just drop them off at the city morgue with that sketchy excuse.

"Yeah, worship was kind of wild today. Anyways, you know your neighbors? Yeah, they died at service today. Are you guys looking for a new church? Would love to welcome you to Jerusalem Christian Center. You don't have to believe before you belong but you might want to believe before you give." [moves Ananias's mouth with hands like a puppet and talks out of side of mouth] "I tried to give without believing and now I'm dead meat!"

Look, this stuff is supposed to temper our theology.

Let this passage bother you.

Let it bring some balance to what may be imbalance.

THAT CORINTHIAN CHURCH

Here we are again, back to the Corinthians. If God is going to kill Christians, He absolutely has a naughty list and this church is on the very top of that list.

We pick up this story in 1 Corinthians 11, where Paul writes one of the funniest Scriptures in the Bible: "in the following directives I have no praise for you, for your meetings do more harm than good" (v. 17 NIV).[67]

Their church is so toxic that it is worse when they gather. I don't think I've ever been to a church service where I thought, *I feel worse for coming here*. Granted, I've been to some gong show services. But never something to this magnitude.

---

67. This verse is emphatic in the Greek text and notes irony. The ESV translates it "But in the following instructions I do not commend you, because when you come together it is not for the better [*kreisson*] but for the worse [*hesson*]." The words "better" (*kreisson*) and "worse" (*hesson*) actually rhyme. This play on words would jar the hearer and drive home their preposterous behavior.

Paul goes on to tell us why this church is such a dumpster fire:

> When you come together, it is not the Lord's supper that you eat. For in eating, each one goes ahead with his own meal. One goes hungry, another gets drunk. What! Do you not have houses to eat and drink in? Or do you despise the church of God and humiliate those who have nothing? What shall I say to you? Shall I commend you in this? No, I will not. (vv. 20–22)

Early church services were typically held in the largest home available. They'd begin with a potluck meal (called the Love Feast) brought by everyone that could afford to bring food[68]; at the end of the meal, bread and wine were taken and the Lord's Supper was observed; as the Eucharist was celebrated and songs were sung in worship, the Holy Spirit would begin to manifest His gifts, and the church would minister to one another; a time of teaching followed this and church was dismissed.

The problem in Corinth, as we read, is that the rich are eating all of the food and drinking all of the wine before the poor can get to the table; the cultural norm was for the rich to eat first and then the poor. Seeing as the

---

68. Leon Morris says, "Clearly at Corinth the Holy Communion was a full meal, of the type called a 'love feast'." See Leon Morris, *1 Corinthians* (Downers Grove, IL: IVP Press, 1985), 156. This was also known as the "agape meal." The Lexham Bible Dictionary says, "the agape meal constituted the earliest-known ritual among Christian churches. Following the pattern of the Last Supper, it included not only a meal of fellowship but also a celebration of the Eucharist." See Jason S. Sturdevant, "Agape Meal" in John D. Barry (ed.) *The Lexham Bible Dictionary* (Bellingham, WA: Lexham Press, 2016).

poor didn't have anything to bring, they are reliant upon the kindness of the rich to share their food. But the rich aren't sharing their food, to the point that they are getting fall-down drunk at church.

One has over-drank and another hasn't had anything.

This is the context of this entire section, and has to be considered as we evaluate what Paul will say next:

> Whoever, therefore, eats the bread or drinks the cup of the Lord in an unworthy manner will be guilty concerning the body and blood of the Lord. Let a person examine himself, then, and so eat of the bread and drink of the cup. For anyone who eats and drinks without discerning the body eats and drinks judgment on himself. That is why many of you are weak and ill, and some have died. But if we judged ourselves truly, we would not be judged. But when we are judged by the Lord, we are disciplined so that we may not be condemned along with the world.
>
> So then, my brothers, when you come together to eat, wait for one another— if anyone is hungry, let him eat at home—so that when you come together it will not be for judgment. (vv. 27–34)

Eating of the table of the Lord in an unworthy manner—contextually here—is to shove your face full of food while your Christian brother is watching you and starving. And you are so out of touch with reality that you don't see it.

Or if I may be even more succinct: eating of the table of the Lord in an unworthy manner is when you make church all about yourself.

It's not about what you can contribute; it's not about what you can bring; it's not about how you can give to the Lord or give to others, enriching their lives. It's all about you.

It's not about God; it's not about His preferences; it's not about how He desires to be worshipped; it's not about His order, but rather your chaos.

The Corinthians are Christian Buddhists who have no desire to inquire about the ways of God. The church is just another place where they can practice self-absorbed spiritually and gorge their souls with everything it can possibly handle.

What they don't realize is that they are filling themselves with sickness.

Paul says that many are sick, and some have died.

Died.

"Dieded," as Georgie says.

In 1 Corinthians 10:16, the chapter before, Paul will call the cup that we drink during Communion "the cup of blessing." This is what is meant by the sacramental language used in sacramental theology, that we don't just merely eat a mid-service snack, a view that Communion has been seemingly relegated to; or that we don't just take these elements as mere symbols for the purpose of remembering. No, here in 1 Corinthians 10–11 there is something much more mystical.

As a Charismatic, I cannot believe we have not embraced the sacramental view of the Eucharist. By sacramental, I mean there is grace that is administered to the recipient of the elements. Powerful grace—grace that is not without effect. Grace that comes from the Presence of the Holy Spirit, who mediates the Presence of Christ to the church.

When I drink the cup, I participate in the Lord's death; by His stripes I'm healed.

He tasted the bitterness of gall so I could taste the sweetness of life to the full.

The blood of Jesus cleanses me from all unrighteousness—but there is more—there is provision in the blood of Jesus, a grace for what He has called me to. I drink the cup like my life depends on it—because it does. And I eat the bread of His broken body, because His body was broken for me, and it is the bread of life—it is manna from heaven that nourishes me in the journey.

When I am eating the bread and drinking the wine, I am saying, "Jesus—You know what I need. Let the Holy Spirit minister the same life that raised You from the dead right now."

This is a deeply powerful magic. Yes, magic. It's the word Lewis would use and it's the word I will use.

And this same magic that cures, kills.

The Corinthians find themselves in a pickle: they

need the bread, but the bread is making them sick; they want the wine, but the wine is killing them. And it's not because there is something wrong with the elements, but rather because there is something wrong with them.

This chapter is so important in this canonical journey we've been on the last two chapters. Because interpreting Old Testament narrative can be dicey. You have to know if the narrative is prescriptive or descriptive. And then you have to see if there are patterns of continuity in the New Testament. And even New Testament narratives can be tricky: just because it's a story in the New Testament doesn't mean it's prescriptive—the book of Acts is full of stories that aren't meant to be replicated.

Are we to take an oath, like Paul, and shave our heads? Are tongues of fire the actual sign of the indwelling Holy Spirit?

What we need to be looking for when building doctrine is clear apostolic teaching: when one of the apostles give really clear instructions and teaching on something, it is safe to build doctrine from what is clear. And the clear interprets the unclear.

When you have people dying at worship services in the Old Testament, and then you have people dying at worship services in the New Testament, and then this entire narrative arc terminates in clear apostolic teaching, what you have is a really solid case.

These aren't biblical one-offs.

These are repeated stories with a New Testament development.

So I think it's important that we sit with these stories

and consider the implications, and if we have a narrow hermeneutic that doesn't allow these Old and New Testament stories (as well as Paul's clear teaching) to say what they mean, we need to toss out our interpretive lens and get another one.

One last New Testament passage to scare us well and good.

In Revelation 2–3, we get a glimpse of Jesus superintending the churches. John sees Jesus walking among the seven candlesticks which are the seven churches, and He's inspecting how good of a job these churches are doing.

Jesus writes a report card for each of the seven churches, and five of them get a failing grade. Jesus says to the Church in Thyatira:

> "These are the words of the Son of God, whose eyes are like blazing fire and whose feet are like burnished bronze. I know your deeds, your love and faith, your service and perseverance, and that you are now doing more than you did at first.

> Nevertheless, I have this against you: You tolerate that woman Jezebel, who calls herself a prophet. By her teaching she misleads my servants into sexual immorality and the eating of food sacrificed to idols. I have given her time to repent of her immorality, but she is unwilling. So I will cast her on a

> bed of suffering, and I will make those who
> commit adultery with her suffer intensely,
> unless they repent of her ways. I will strike
> her children dead. Then all the churches
> will know that I am he who searches hearts
> and minds, and I will repay each of you
> according to your deeds." (2:18–23 NIV)

Um, yikes.

This is the risen Jesus here. And He speaks to a Christian Buddhist who calls herself spiritual but is living her own life and writing her own rules and completely disregarding the will of God as revealed in Scripture on the matters of immorality and idolatry.

It's all about her. She is the authority, but she is about to experience another authority.

Jesus threatens to "cast her on a bed of suffering" and cause others to "suffer intensely"; Jesus then says that He will strike her children dead (probably means her spiritual offspring).

Is it really faithful to the text to paint God as someone who is wishy-washy about holiness?

Is it really faithful to the text—after everything we've read—to suggest that Christians are somehow *unpunishable*? Is that even remotely orthodox?

Is it really faithful to the text to suggest that God is never retributive in His judgment—that He's always restorative and never just zaps someone? How do we make sense of Acts 5 and 1 Corinthians 11, then?

No, I think it's dangerous to project onto God our

modern feelings and cultural sensitivities, and force Scripture to wrap around our prior ideological commitments that we hope will win a confused world led about by whatever seems to feel good at the time.

I think it's dangerous—as we have seen—to pretend that the truth exists as we see it and not externally to us.

Every one of these people who died at a worship service experienced truth as phenomenologically transcendent. If you don't believe that a tree is real, and you think it's a mist or a giant beach ball or a portal into Narnia, and you drive your car through that tree, you will experience phenomenological transcendence.

A collision with the reality of a holy God who has painstakingly revealed Himself is not the best way to learn about or encounter God. The best way is to learn from others—from God's self-revelation through His interactions with other human beings.

Christian, you have the advantage. You can take God at His Word and know Him. You can eat of the Tree of Life or you can eat of the Tree of the Knowledge of Good and Evil, and build your own spiritual journey.

I love what Wayne Grudem says: "Even though we cannot know God exhaustively, we can know true things about God."[69]

When I die and go to heaven, I'm not going to look up at God and think, *Okay, I've figured You out.* God is eternal, immortal, invisible—I am an ant compared to His intelligence. The mystery of His greatness will forever blow my mind in eternity. Eternity will not exhaust or even scratch

---

69. Wayne Grudem, *Systematic Theology* (Grand Rapids: Zondervan, 2004), 151.

the surface of the incalculability of His glory.

I'm never gonna know everything there is to know about God, but I can know Him accurately. I don't have to scratch my head and figure this God thing out by myself. God has revealed Himself perfectly. It is my job, now, to respond to that revelation.

Jesus said, "The Father is looking for those who will worship in spirit and truth."[70]

Humans don't seem to have a problem with that spirit part, but we bristle at the truth part, because truth means that we aren't in control.

But this is how we offer acceptable worship, and this is what the Father is looking for.

---

70. See John 4:23.

Chapter Twelve

INVITATION TO A BONFIRE

Growing up in Canada, we used to host and attend bonfires quite often. Summer nights were often spent around a campfire—even our summers weren't that hot. Aside from smelling like smoke the next day, I can honestly say that I've enjoyed every campfire I've ever been to.

I love the hotdogs on sticks, the flaming marshmallows sandwiched between two graham crackers and a slice of chocolate, and the comforting crackle of logs being consumed in the flames. Never in my life have I ever had a nervous thought about campfires, because I respect fire.

My dad taught me a fear of fire at a very young age; I was terrified of the oven, careful around the toaster, and anxious around microwaves. My younger brother melted his hand on a lawnmower engine when he was three and that heightened my paranoia of hot things.

In high school, the hockey team would have a huge bonfire on the winter weekends, drink a bazillion beers, and then jump over the fire. There isn't much to do in rural Canada during the winter, I suppose. I remember coming to school one day and word around the cafeteria was that one of the guys fell into the fire, drunk off his head, when he was trying to jump. His jacket, hair, and hands had been singed—mostly his pride was hurt.

Other than those boys, I'd never even heard of anyone getting hurt at a bonfire, because for the most part, people fear fire—and that keeps them safe.

Fire is a bit peripheral to society nowadays—we don't really use it like we used to. I'm writing this chapter on a Dreamliner over the Pacific, propelled by four giant fans, each powered by a combustible engine—fire. Should that fire die out, we will have to make a water landing. Fire is keeping me alive right now.

Trains, planes, automobiles—sparks in the form of electricity that power basically everything—all of our lives are powered by small controlled flames. And we take the danger of it all for granted because of how well insulated our products are from its potential for devastation.

I never think that my iPhone is powered by being plugged into a socket in the wall—a socket that I could access carelessly with a butter knife for a jolly jolt.

I never get into my car and fear the controlled explosions that are happening every second I step on the gas.

There are protections in place that harness the life of the flame.

The book of Hebrews says that God is a consuming fire. The author writes, "Therefore, since we are receiving a kingdom that can't be shaken, let us be thankful, and so worship God acceptably with reverence and awe, for our 'God is a consuming fire'" (12:28–29 NIV).

The context of God being a consuming fire is one that is calling the Hebrews to acceptable forms of worship—worship that God has asked for. And the author is suggesting that acceptable worship has a reverence and an awe because God is dangerous—He's a consuming fire.[71]

God is not described as being a soft pillow.

This verse is meant to put a bit of fear into us.

And this is what Lewis means when Mr. Beaver responds to Lucy about Aslan the lion:

> "Safe?" said Mr. Beaver; "don't you hear what Mrs. Beaver tells you? Who said anything about safe? 'Course he isn't safe. But he's good. He's the King, I tell you."[72]

God is good.

And like fire, all of life flows from Him, the source of life that keeps the lights on.

Now, I've written these words in the cultural context of a Western Christianity that views God like an indentured servant, an obligated father who has to pay child support, except that He gets to take care of us because He's obsessed with us.

---

71. Donald Guthrie notes the words of Hebrews 12:29 echoes the words of Deuteronomy 4:24. He says, "This awe-inspiring view of God takes its colouring from the Sinai event. It is a reminder that even the believer in Christ must recognize that the character of God is righteous and that his character will not change. Even although the epistle ends on a softer note (cf. 13:20), this sense of the awesomeness of God cannot be dispensed with, but should inculcate a true sense of reverence." See Donald Guthrie, *Hebrews* (Downers Grove, IL: IVP Press, 1983), 266.
72. C. S. Lewis, *The Chronicles of Narnia: The Lion, The Witch, and the Wardrobe* (Grand Rapids: Zondervan, 2009), 146.

I'm writing in the context of a church culture that has taken the idea of God's love and mercy and grace so far that we have never even heard most of these Scriptures before. We seldom consider God to be someone who would insist on "acceptable worship" as both Peter and the author of Hebrews suggest.

The idea that there would be death in the New Testament church is as foreign as it is absurd in our love-obsessed church cultures.

And yet, there it is.

Now, I've not written this book to say, "Sometimes God kills people."

That's simply not what I'm getting at, although that certainly must be part of the equation.

What I'm saying is, don't act like an idiot at a bonfire.

Pay God as much respect as you pay a fire.

You don't relate to fire on your terms; you relate to it on its terms.

There is no negotiating with a flame. It exists as it is, and we exist as we are, and if we are to benefit from the relationship, we are the ones that have to change—not it.

I can either be warmed by the fire, or burned by the fire, but I will encounter the fire, and I live by the fire—the fire powers all.

And this has never stopped to be the reality of the church throughout history. Christians are healed or sickened by their worship; they are revived or rebuked—the church burgeons or busts—by the state of their worship.

The catastrophe of our postmodern ecclesial ills—*Deconstruction* (the Derridean word we've attempted to baptize, a modern portmanteau for Paul's "shipwreck," the way of the mainline denominations that have become anathema), *destruction* (the hijacking and fracturing of churches by consumers), and *derision* brought on by the divisiveness of woke politics—these are all worship issues.

Rejecting historic Christian readings of Scripture in lieu of more culturally favorable doctrines on human sexuality is a worship issue: it's offering strange fire. If Deconstruction were a return to Scripture in the spirit of the Reformation, I would be on board. But it is not, because it is a rejection of both reliable methodology[73] as well as Scripture as the foundation for knowing God.

The result of Deconstruction is worship that is not in truth—worship that is rejected and a worshipper that is rejected.

The problem of the consumer is much more troubling depending on the depth of the self-deceit, because at least the deconstructor leaves the church; the consumer stays and hijacks the purpose of the church, like the drunk Corinthian who despises his brother and thus despises God. That is a much worse problem.

As I said before, the title of this book isn't *Sometimes God Kills People*, because that's really not how you invite someone to a bonfire.

You never include a legal qualifier: it is assumed that people understand the danger of fire, and act accordingly. It would sound ridiculous and rude and contradictory to the whole point of a bonfire if you spelled it right out.

---

73. For a crash course on method and hermeneutics, see the book we use in our hermeneutics courses at Theos Seminary: William W. Klein, Craig L. Blomberg, and Robert L. Hubbard Jr., *Introduction to Biblical Interpretation, Third Edition* (Grand Rapids: Zondervan, 2017).

"Look—we're having a bonfire on Friday night and we want you to come over, but we just want to warn you: fire is hot. It could melt your flesh in seconds. Have you ever seen burn victims? It's messed up, right? Anyways, come over and hang with us Friday—at your own peril."

Bonfire culture has this built-in democratic anxiety about people getting burned. Whenever a kid runs a little too close, or if someone walks by too quickly, or if a flame jumps out because the wind turns—about four different people are gonna shout or say something quickly.

The Evangelical church doesn't have a built-in warning system anymore like the nervous fire watchers.

In the nineties, people who totally rejected Christian sexual ethics just left. They knew better than to stay around—once it came to that, they were done with Christianity. They knew there were things they disagreed with and they just walked. And we let them.

Nowadays we're always chasing the "Rich Young Ruler," begging him to stay.

"Dude, no, come back. You can 'journey' with us, even though that will cause all kinds of division in our staff and team over the course of the next five years, and half of my people won't believe a word that comes out of my mouth anymore because all I care about is butts in seats."

So when you say it, it comes as an absolute shock.

God is a consuming fire?

"How could you possibly read 1 Corinthians 11 and believe people could be sick as a result of failed worship? That's not the Jesus that I know."

Tell me about the Jesus that you know: Did you find

Him in Scripture? And how does the Jesus you know get rounded out by John's Jesus, both in his Gospel and in Revelation?

A WAY FORWARD

Here's what I'm proposing: that we continue to invite people to the bonfire, but explain what is happening.

Teaching the Bible is how we protect people from being burned.

It's how David addressed the Uzzah incident; it's where he drew the confidence to boldly dance before the Presence like a maniac. The Scriptures understood and applied give confidence, not lack thereof.

Somehow we've become embarrassed of this spiritual reality, but I think it's because we've lost the concept entirely—like in the days of King David. I see the church throughout history as having the ark, losing the ark, being wounded by the ark, losing the ark, regaining the ark, and on and on. There are moments of church history that are bright; and there are moments where the ability to handle the Presence seems lost for a century.

We have to begin to teach what is at stake again. We have good-hearted leaders—King Davids—who desire the Presence of God and will do anything to bring it into the temple, but don't know how to steward it. We have church movements that have stewarded it and have lost it because they didn't understand its stewardship.

I'm watching modern church movements lose young Christians and leaders—not because they aren't woke enough, but because there is no fear of God; and these young people aren't leaving, they're sick; they have become Corinthian in their factions, focus, and selfishness. They are ignorant of the Scriptures, which are able to make them wise unto salvation.

Their God consciousness has been eclipsed by their cultural consciousness.

Their priestly identity is second to their political identity.

God and the church must serve them.

They are drunk on the wine of idolatry.

The cure is to address their idolatry and low ecclesiology, not sidestep their sickness.

The Holy Spirit is the one who illumines the Word. When I describe God as a consuming fire who demands reverential acts of worship that are acceptable, and I accurately represent the reality of Scripture, the Spirit does a work in the heart.

When I shy away from these theological realities, there is no root of the fear of the Lord. I have become partner in the rootlessness of this generation.

So invite them to the glory of God. Tell them about the benefits of true worship: emphasize the life and vitality of God's Presence. Let that be the earmark of our churches, but let us not fail to accurately portray the consequences of treating a holy God and His directives for worship with contempt.

They must know who may ascend the hill of the Lord.

And we can't be sidetracked by pet sins that we tend to slam, either. Sexual sin is not the biggest fire that we need to warn people about.

Rather, it's thinking that you can construct God in any way that seems fitting; assuming that the church of Jesus Christ exists to serve you; and the pride of thinking that you have no sin. Those are the biggies.

This is my great concern for the deconstructing "Christians" who affirm sexual sin: they are offering strange fire.

It's not the sin itself—it's the refusal to call it what God calls it. A priest does not tell God what incense will go in his censer.

This is my great concern for the consumer who has become drunk on their own spiritual journey, shredding the church to bits and never joining a community to actually contribute: they are eating of the table of the Lord in an unworthy manner.

This is my great concern for deconstructing "Christians" who are calling the God of the Old Testament a moral monster, making Jesus a social liberator, and reviling Paul as uninspired. They have put the ark on a theological wooden cart, and they have ignored how the Presence ought to be carried because they have rejected what Scripture means in favor of expediency.

"Just put the ark on a cart, it's fine."

And I believe the Holy Spirit—through Scripture—is saying, "No more ox carts."

We must return to what the Lord has said about the church—about her purpose. We have to remind the people they are priests, not consumers. Knowing the fear of the Lord, we must persuade our people to worship God His way: in spirit and truth.

We can no longer hide parts of the Bible that we aren't proud of.

We have to stop chasing the Rich Young Ruler. Let him walk away at the hard sayings of Christ—but for the love of God, tell him the words of Christ.

Worship must be understood as the chief activity of the church—acceptable worship offered in reverence and awe to our God, who is a consuming fire.

The church must welcome God to His temple, priests to the altar, and sinners to a bonfire.

BIBLIOGRAPHY

Aquinas, Thomas. *Summa Theologica*. Translated by Fathers of the English Dominican Province. London: Burns Oates & Washbourne, n.d.

Bavnick, Herman. *The Doctrine of God*, translated and edited by William Hendrickson. Grand Rapids: Eerdmans, 1951, 86–89.

Beale, G. K. *Handbook on the New Testament Use of the Old Testament*. Grand Rapids: Baker Academic, 2012, 31.

Beale. G. K. and David Campbell. *Revelation: A Shorter Commentary*. Grand Rapids: Eerdmans, 2015, 168.

Behm, Johannes. "θύω, θυσία, θυσιαστήριον." In Gerhard Kittel, Geoffrey W. Bromiley, and Gerhard Friedrich, eds. *Theological Dictionary of the New Testament*. Grand Rapids: Eerdmans, 1964, 180–90.

Block, Daniel I. *For the Glory of God: Recovering a Biblical Theology of Worship*. Grand Rapids: Baker Academic, 2016, 23.

Borchert, Gerald L. *John 1–11*. Nashville: Broadman & Holman Publishers, 1996, 154–55.

Brown-Driver-Briggs Hebrew and English Lexicon. Peabody, MA: Hendrickson, 1996, 872–73.

Bruce, F. F. *Romans: An Introduction and Commentary*. Downers Grove, IL: IVP Academic, 1985, 250.

Carson, D. A. *Exegetical Fallacies, Second Edition*. Grand Rapids: Baker Books, 1996.

———. *The Gospel According to John*. Grand Rapids: Eerdmans, 1991, 123, 170, 358.

Chesterton, G. K. *Orthodoxy*. New York: John Lane Company, 1908, 85.

Ciampa, Roy E. and Brian S. Rosner. *The First Letter to the Corinthians*. Grand Rapids: Eerdmans, 2010.

Culver, Robert D. "Anoint, Anointed." In Walter A. Elwell, ed. *Baker Encyclopedia of the Bible, Vol. 1*. Grand Rapids: Baker Book House, 1988, 116.

Damazio, Frank. "The Anointing Value." Passions and Values (class lecture, Portland Bible College, April 10, 2008).

———. *The Gate Church*. Portland, OR: City Christian Publishing, 2003.

———. *The Making of a Leader.* Portland, OR: City Bible Publishing, 1988, 283–300.

France, R. T. *Matthew: An Introduction and Commentary.* Downers Grove, IL: IVP Press, 1985, 325.

Freedman, David Noel, ed. *Eerdmans Dictionary of the Bible.* Grand Rapids: Eerdmans, 2000, 388.

Greene, Gene L. *The Letters to the Thessalonians.* Grand Rapids: Eerdmans, 2002, 18–19.

Grudem, Wayne. *Systematic Theology: An Introduction to Bible Doctrine, Second Edition.* Grand Rapids: Zondervan Academic, 2020, 269–82.

Guthrie, Donald. *Hebrews: An Introduction and Commentary.* Grand Rapids: Wm. B. Eerdmans, 1983.

Jewett, Robert. *Romans: A Commentary on the Book of Romans.* Minneapolis: Augsburg Fortress, 2007, 353.

Jung, C. G. *Introduction to Jungian Psychology: Notes of the Seminar on Analytical Psychology Given in 1923.* Princeton, NJ: Princeton University Press, 2012.

Klein, William W., Craig L. Blomberg, and Robert L. Hubbard Jr. *Introduction to Biblical Interpretation, Third Edition.* Grand Rapids: Zondervan, 2017.

Kruse, Colin G. *Romans.* Pillar New Testament Commentary Series. Grand Rapids: Eerdmans, 2012, 435.

Lachs, John. "Transcendence in Philosophy and Everyday Life." *The Journal of Speculative Philosophy* 11, no. 4 (1997): 247–55.

Lanier, Gregory R. "Glory." In Douglas Magnum, ed. et al. *Lexham Theological Workbook*, Lexham Bible Reference Series. Bellingham, WA: Lexham Press, 2014.

Levin, Yuval. *The Fractured Republic: Renewing America's Social Contract in the Age of Individualism.* New York: Basic Books, 2017, 148.

Lewis, C. S. *God in the Dock: Essays on Theology and Ethics.* Edited by Walter Hooper. Grand Rapids: Eerdmans, 1970, 217–25.

———. *The Chronicles of Narnia: The Lion, The Witch, and the Wardrobe.* Grand Rapids: Zondervan, 2009, 146.

Luther, Martin. "To the Christian Nobility of the German Nation." In *Luther's Works*, 44:129.

MacArthur, John. *1 Corinthians.* The MacArthur New Testament Commentary. Chicago: Moody, 1984, vii.

Madvig, D. H. "Corinth." In *International Standard Bible Encyclopedia*, vol. 1. Grand Rapids: Eerdmans, 1994, 773.

McDowell, John et al. *What D. L. Moody Means to Me: An Anthology of Appreciations and Appraisals of the Beloved Founder of the Northfield Schools.* E. Northfield, MA: The Northfield Schools, 1931, 23. In Lyle W. Dorsett. *A Passion for Souls: The Life of D. L. Moody.* Chicago: Moody Publishers, 1997, 19.

Morris, Leon. *1 and 2 Thessalonians.* Downers Grove, IL: IVP Press, 1984, 37.

————. *1 Corinthians.* Downers Grove, IL: IVP Press, 1985,156.

Peterson, David G. *The Acts of the Apostles.* Grand Rapids: Eerdmans, 2009, 208–9.

Rollinson, Philip B., Douglas F. Kelly, and Frederick T. Marsh. *The Westminster Shorter Catechism in Modern English.* Phillipsburg, NJ: Presbyterian and Reformed Pub. Co., 1986, 1.

Rudolph, Kurt. "Gnosticism." In *Anchor Bible Dictionary.* Edited by David Noel Freedman. New York: Doubleday, 1992, 1033–40.

Schloemann, Martin. *Luthers Apfelbäumchen: Ein Kapitel deutscher Mentalitätsgeschichte seit dem Zweiten Weltkrieg.* Göttingen: Vandenhoeck & Ruprecht, 1994, 246–51.

Steinmetz, Katy. "She Coined the Term 'Intersectionality'

Over 30 Years Ago. Here's What It Means to Her Today." *TIME*, February 20, 2020. https://time.com/5786710/kimberle-crenshaw-intersectionality/.

Wallace, Daniel B. *Greek Grammar Beyond the Basics.* Grand Rapids: Zondervan, 1996, 530–31.

Waltke, Bruce. *An Old Testament Theology: An Exegetical, Canonical, and Thematic Approach*. Grand Rapids: Zondervan, 2007, 27.

Woudstra, Marten H. "Ark of the Covenant." In *Baker Encyclopedia of the Bible*. Edited by Walter A. Elwell. Grand Rapids: Baker Book House, 1988, 169–72.

Zahnd, Brian. *When Everything's on Fire: Faith Forged from the Ashes.* Downers Grove, IL: IVP Press, 2021, 26.

ACKNOWLEDGMENTS

Thank you to Chris Palmer, who encouraged me to write this book and helped me tremendously with research; to Whitney Gossett, a faithful friend and book genius, helping me to organize my energy; and Amanda Varian, for making my manuscript intelligible.

ABOUT THE AUTHOR

Nathan Finochio is the Founder of TheosU and Theos Seminary, the author of *Hearing God: Eliminate Myths, Encounter Meaning* (Waterbrook), and lives in Palm Desert, California, with his wife, Jasmine.

9 781954 020290